A DESCRIPTIVE GRAMMAR *of* ENGLISH

BY EXAMPLE

Andrew Rossiter

Linguapress

ISBN-13: 978 - 2958385507
Revision 2.2 (2023)
This hardback edition (revision 2.0.1) first published 2022

Originally published in paperback 2020 (revision 1.0).
Copyright © Andrew Rossiter. All rights reserved. No part of this publication may be reproduced, stored in a retrievable system, or transmitted in any form or by any means without the prior permission of the copyright-holder.
Linguapress.com
Publishing through IngramSpark

This book is also available in French
 Nouvelle grammaire descriptive de l'anglais. ISBN 979 - 8650107736

Reviews

"A *Descriptive Grammar of English by Example* should be included on your list of reference material…. This book is a huge step forward, and having the English language laid out in such a user-friendly approach is a welcome treat for non-native teachers and learners."
IATEFL Voices magazine,

"Overall, this is a useful reference book to have on hand when planning for and teaching grammar lessons. The clarity of explanations and wealth of examples, alongside helpful visual keys, provide both new and experienced teachers with something easy to dip into, regardless of the language level they are teaching."
EFL Magazine,

The author

Andrew Rossiter, now retired from active teaching, was for many years course coordinator and chair of the department of Applied Languages at the University of Franche-Comté in Besançon, France.

After graduating from the University of Edinburgh with an honours degree in modern languages, and following a doctorate in literature, he spent most of his career teaching in universities in France, specialising in English language and contemporary British area studies. He has also been guest lecturer at universities in the UK, Spain and Italy.

Over thirty years of teaching experience have provided him with a broad-ranging insight into the difficulties of the English language, as perceived by speakers of different languages as well as by native English speakers.

He has contributed articles to leading English language teaching periodicals including the *ELT Journal* and *EL Gazette* in the UK, *Les Langues Modernes* (France), *Engels* (the Netherlands), *AngloFiles* (Denmark) and others.

He was founding editor of the innovative Linguapress language-learning newsmagazines, which were widely used in schools and colleges throughout Europe before the age of the omnipresent Internet, and remains on the board of the French National Association for Applied Languages.

Preface to the hardback edition 2022

Grammar; why is it controversial?

Last year I had an interesting exchange of emails with Debra Myhill, Professor of Education at the University of Exeter, and vice-president of the UK Literary Association. To my suggestion that people in English-speaking countries had a cultural hangup and antipathy towards grammar, Professor Myhill replied. "I very much agree.... The minute grammar is mentioned, reason flies out the window and polemicism rushes through the door.... generating an ever-recycled set of arguments for and arguments against..."

For Myhill, the contrast with attitudes to the teaching of English grammar in other countries was sharp. "I have led some professional development courses in other countries and it has been lovely to focus on teaching about how grammar can provide insight into how language works and find that the teachers are all so confident with the underlying grammar!"

That set me thinking. I'd originally imagined this book as a handbook for students – whether native English speakers or learners of English as a second or foreign language. Years of hands-on experience teaching grammar to students from high school to postgraduate levels had convinced me of the need for an up-to-date compact pedagogical reference grammar of English, giving priority to a clear and pragmatic expression of the main rules, and designed principally for students. But teachers?

Are there many teachers, notably native speakers, as well as students, who feel ill at ease with English grammar? It seems that the answer to this question is "yes", and maybe this is actually to be expected, given the story of English grammar over the past half century.

From the late 1960s onwards, the formal teaching of English grammar was largely phased out of the education programmes in the main English-speaking countries, to the point where in some areas and for some years "grammar" was not officially taught at all. In some circles, the teaching of grammar was (and indeed still is) deemed elitist, as if grammar were something that only the elite were able to understand, or that there was something elitist in being able to use English to express meanings correctly and without ambiguity. That might have been the case in the eighteenth century; but in the twenty-first, in the age of communication and interpersonal skills, the ability to speak and write English coherently is a skill that should definitely not be the reserved domain of an elite.

By the 1990s the teaching of grammar had become a problem, even in the world of EFL / ESL where grammar remained more in fashion than in the world of first language teaching. It was not that teachers did not see the need for grammar; it was increasingly due to the new reality that young teachers starting out in the late twentieth century felt unable or unqualified to teach grammar, having themselves come through school with little or no grammar training in the curriculum; this continued into the early years of the twenty-first century. And if there is one truth that underlies all teaching, it is that you can't teach something effectively if you don't really understand it yourself.

So maybe one of the reasons why the teaching of English grammar remains a controversial topic is not that many teachers cannot or do not want to teach it, or do not see the use of doing so, but the fact that grammar is something with which they themselves do not feel at ease. And when teachers are not confident with English grammar, it is hardly surprising that they will either hesitate to mention it in the classroom, or else if they do so, will pass on their own confusions to their students.

The aim of this book is thus – as EL Gazette put it – to "demystify grammar"; and the first step towards doing this is to point out that "Grammar" is not an exact science, but a system for describing language use. In this respect it is to a large extent what teachers and students make it; and it can be made frighteningly complex when confused with linguistics (which is how it may appear to students who see it in terms of the classic 1800-page linguistic grammars of English studied at university), or relatively simple.... which in most cases it really is.

When it comes to teaching and learning grammar effectively, there are two essential rules to follow. The first is to concentrate on the basics, and the second is to make full use of relevant and clear examples. Language acquisition at all levels involves listening, mimicry and adaptation; this is how children first learn to speak, and – in a different paradigm – how older learners and other language learners acquire their skills. And across the full range of language usage, if there is one skill that is fundamental to the development of virtually all aspects of expression and comprehension, and thus of literacy itself, it is an awareness of grammar.

Why then does the teaching of grammar remain controversial in some quarters? Could it really be down to a fear of the unknown?

Andrew Rossiter   France 2022

Table of Contents

1. Verbs

1.1. Verbs: **What are verbs?** 1.1.1. Verbs in the sentence
   1.1.2. Different types of verb   1.1.3. Tense, aspect, voice
   1.1.4. Modality   1.1.5. Moods   1.1.6 The subjunctive 5

1.2. Verbs: **Present tenses**   1.2.1. Different types of present tense
   1.2.2. The simple present   1.2.3. The present progressive.................9

1.3. Verbs: **Expressing the future** 1.3.1. Forms of the future
   1.3.2. The present tense used as a future tense
   1.3.3. *Will* and *going to*   1.3.4. *Shall*
   1.3.5. Negative forms   1.3.6. Other forms of the future......................12

1.4. Verbs: **Expressing the past** 1.4.1. Forms of past tenses
   1.4.2. The Simple past   1.4.3. The present perfect
   1.4.4. The past perfect   1.4.6. The future perfect............................15

1.5. Verbs: **Conditional structures** with *if* or *unless*
   1.5.1. Conditional clauses   1.5.2. Open *if* clauses
   1.5.3. The open hypothesis 1.5.4. The unfulfilled hypothesis
   1.5.5. Omission of *if*   1.5.6. *Whether* 18

1.6. Verbs: **The infinitive** 1.6.1. Short infinitives   1.6.2. Full infinitives
   with *to* 1.6.3. Past infinitives   1.6.4. Passive infinitives   1.6.5.
   Infinitive or gerund? 1.6.6. Other points   1.6.7. Split infinitives 22

1.7. Verbs: **The imperative** 1.7.1. Uses of the imperative   1.7.2. Forms
   of the imperative, soft imperatives 1.7.3. Emphatic imperatives 28

1.8. Verbs: **Active and passive** 1.8.1 Usage   1.8.2. The passive for
   emphasis 1.8.3. The passive for impersonal statements 1.8.4. The
   passive to simplify sentence structure 1.8.5. Forms of the passive
   1.8.6. The passive followed by an object...30

1.9. Verbs: **Gerunds and -*ing* forms** 1.9.1. Different types of word
   ending in -*ing*   1.9.2. Gerunds 1.9.3. Verbal nouns   1.9.4. Areas
   of confusion
   1.9.5. Present participles 1.9.6. -*ing* forms in passive structures 34

1.10. Consecutive verbs - -***ing* or an infinitive**
   1.10.1. Gerund or infinitive? 39

1.11. ***To be***: Forms of *to be* 1.11.1. Functions – main verb
   1.11.2. Functions – auxiliary verb 1.11.3. Passive forms with *be*
   1.11.4. Progressive tenses in the passive 1.11.5. *Get* used in place
   of *be* 1.11.6. Avoid confusion 1.11.7. *To be* as a modal verb 41

1.12. *To* **have**: 1.12.1. *Have* as a main verb, - forms, abbreviated forms, negative forms 1.12.2. *Have* or *have got* ? 1.12.3. *Have* as an auxiliary verb – forms, contracted forms and negative forms 46

1.13. **Do** and **make**: uses and differences 1.13.1. Meanings 1.13.2 *Do* – uses and expressions 1.13.3 *Make* - functions and usage 52

1.14. **Get** and **got**: 1.14.1. Forms of *get* 1.14.1. *Get* as a main verb 1.14.2. Phrasal and prepositional uses 1.14.3. *Get* as a passive auxiliary 56

1.15. **Modal verbs of obligation** - *must, should, ought to, need to* 1.15.1. Firm obligation, *must* & *have to* 1.15.2. Recommendation or moral obligation *should* & *ought to* , and *need (to)*..58

1.16 **Modal verbs of ability** - *can, could, may* and *might*. 1.16.1. Open possibility *can could* & *be able to* 1.16.2. Potential possibility, authority – *may* & *might*.. 62

1.17. Verbs of **enabling & obligation** - *allow, let, prevent* etc 1.17.1. Obligation and authority 1.17.2. Prevention 1.17.3. Causative verbs *let make have* 66

1.18. **Phrasal & prepositional** verbs How to distinguish between them 1.18.1. Separable or inseparable? 1.18.2. Transitive verbs 1.18.3. Intransitive verbs 1.18.4. Special cases & exceptions 68

1.19. **Irregular** verbs General principles...73

2. The Noun phrase

2.1. **Nouns** : What is a noun? 2.1.1. Classification of nouns 2.1.2. Nouns and gender 2.1.3. The formation of nouns 2.1.4. Nouns in the plural 2.1.5. Collective nouns 74

2.2. **Noun phrases**   Types of noun phrase 2.2.1 Composition 2.2.2. Modifiers in noun phrases   2.2.3. Exceptions 81

2.3. **Count and non-count** nouns 2.3.1. Count nouns 2.3.2. Non-count nouns 2.3.3. Usage 2.3.4. Nouns that can be countable or uncountable 2.3.5. Quantifiers with count & non-count nouns................................83

2.4. **Pronouns** 1: Definition 2.4.1. **Personal** pronouns , including *one*, reflexive pronouns, emphatic pronouns, indefinite pronouns, gender-neutral pronouns, and *there* as a pronoun............................87

2.4.2. Pronouns 2: **Relative** pronouns and adjectives functions and forms, Nominal relative pronouns, Relative adjectives, *why, when* & *how* 2.4.3. Relative adverb - *however*..91

2.4.4 Pronouns 3: Demonstrative pronouns *this that these those* 95
2.5. Articles 2.5.1. Usage
    2.5.2. The definite article *the*   2.5.3. Indefinite articles *a an*
    2.5.4. Is an article necessary? 2.5.5. Articles & quantifiers................98
2.6. Quantifiers   Definition – 2.6.1. *some, any, no* & their compounds
    2.6.2. Large quantity quantifiers *Much, many lots of* etc.
    2.6.3. Small quantity quantifiers – *few, a few, little* etc.
    2.6.4. Neutral and relative quantity quantifiers - *some, each, all, whole most* etc. 2.6.5. Quantifiers followed by *of* 100
2.7. Numbers and counting 2.7.1. Cardinal numbers 113
    2.7.2. Ordinals 117
    2.7.3. Fractions and decimals 119
2.8. Possession Using *of* or *'s*
    2.8.1. Animates, human possessors
    2.8.2. Inanimate possessors 121
2.9. Adjectives in English, Definition 2.9.1. Determining adjectives
    2.9.2. Descriptive adjectives, qualifying or classifying
    2.9.3. Usage – attributive or predicative   2.9.4. Plural adjectives
    2.9.5. The formation of adjectives   2.9.6. Comparison of adjectives
    2.9.7. The gradation of adjectives 2.9.8. Adjective order.................125

3. Other parts of speech

3.1. **Adverbs** in English   3.1.1. Two families of adverb
    3.1.2. Adverbs related to adjectives
    3.1.3. Adverbs unrelated to adjectives
    3.1.4. Sentence adverbs..132
3.2. **Prepositions** Definition
3.2.1. Prepositions of position & direction   3.2.2. Prepositions of time
    3.2.3. Manner & other relations   3.2.4 Other prepositions
    3.2.5. End a sentence with a preposition...137
3.3. **Conjunctions** and connectors. Definition
    3.3.1. Coordinating conjunctions *but and nor yet or*
    3.3.1.2. Starting a sentence with a conjunction
    3.3.2. Subordinating conjunctions including *that* 3.3.3. Examples
    3.3.4. *So* as a coordinating conjunction
    3.3.5. Correlating coordinators (*both… and, either… or* etc)...........143
3.4. **Conjunctive adverbs** such as *however* or *therefore*
    3.4.1. Definition – the nature of conjunctive adverbs
    3.4.2. Usage 149

4. Sentences and clauses

4.1. Word order in **statements**
   4.1.1. Subject verb and direct object
   4.1.2. Other elements including indirect objects and adverb phrases 4.1.3. Complex or compound sentences 153

4.2. Word order in **questions** Essential question structure
   4.2.1. Question words or *wh*-words
   4.2.2. Questions with single word verbs 4.2.3. Exceptions.............. 157

4.3. **Reported questions** Reported questions and verb tenses
   4.3.1. Reporting the present – simultaneous reporting
   4.3.2. Reporting the past – deferred reporting
   4.3.3. Absolute and relative adverbs of time and place 159

4.4. **Tag questions** 4.4.1. Definitions and functions
   4.4.2. Structure of tag questions 4.4.3. Formation and use of tags.
   4.4.4. Alternative forms of negative tags... 163

4.5. **Negative** structures Different ways of expressing negation in English
   4.5.1. Negative forms of the verb 4.5.2. Negating with a quantifier
   4.5.3. Negation using a noun or pronoun
   4.5.4. Negation using an adverb or adverb phrase
   4.5.5. *neither… nor* – linking negative elements 4.5.6. Negation using negative adjectives   4.5.7. Negation and tag questions....... 167

4.6. **Relative clauses** Forms and functions
   4.6.1. The relative pronoun as subject
   4.6.2. The relative pronoun as object   4.6.3. *Whose*
   4.6.4. Relative clauses starting with a preposition
   4.6.5. More complex structures 4.6.6. Defining and non-defining relative clauses 4.6.7. Using *that* instead of *who* or *which*
   4.6.8 Relative clauses qualifying a whole sentence
   4.6.9. Omission of the relative pronoun 172

4.7. **Punctuation**.. 178

4.8. **Language and style**... 184

5.   **Glossary** of essential grammar terms.. 188

Note: Use of colour in this book.
This grammar makes extensive use of **colour coding**. Generally speaking **dark red** colour is used to highlight the **key words** in any paragraph. When other colours are used, such as scarlet or blue or green, these are essentially to contrast different structures or different categories, or to relate contrastive examples to different cases.

1. Verbs in English
1.1. What are verbs and how are they used?

Verbs are among the essential building blocks of communication in any language. They are one of the two essential elements of a sentence or clause. The other is the subject.

> **Verbs: a definition**
>
> A **verb** exists in relation to a **subject**. It is the key and essential element of the **predicate** in a sentence. The verb expresses an action or process undertaken by or undergone by the subject, or a situation defining the subject.
>
> **Actions**: to break, to start, to shout
>
> **Processes**: to sleep, to eat, to think
>
> **Situations**: to be, to seem, to live

1.1.1. Verbs in the sentence

Every sentence is made up of a **subject** and **a predicate**. The predicate must contain a **verb**, and can contain many other elements too (a complement, an object or more, adverbs, circumstantial expressions, etc.).

Examples

- The president sneezed.
- You have taken the wrong bag.
- The man and the woman both forgot.
- He forgot to get off the train at York.

1.1.2. Different types of verb

Transitive or intransitive?

Verbs can either be **transitive** or **intransitive**.
- A transitive verb **requires** an object.
- An intransitive verb **cannot have** an object.

Some verbs can be transitive or intransitive, depending on context.

Examples

> **Transitive:** to send, to employ, to like, to tell
> **Intransitive**: to sleep, to die, to happen
> **Verbs that can be either**: to give, to burn, to smell

Stative or dynamic?

Verbs can be either **stative** or **dynamic**. Stative verbs describe a situation or state, dynamic verbs describe a process or change of state. The two categories are incompatible with each other.

Stative - describing a state: *to know, to lie, to be, to like,*

Dynamic - expressing a change of state: *to discover, to lie down, to become, to learn.*

Examples

> 1) I **know** a lot of people in London.
> 2) My father **likes** beer but not whisky.
> 3) That box **weighs** over twenty kilos.
> 4) Who **does** this phone **belong** to?
> 5) The scientists **discovered** a new planet on the edge of the solar system.
> 6) I **sat down** and **went** to sleep.
> 7) The price **has increased** by ten euros.
> 8) **Have** you **bought** a new bike?

1.1.3. Tense, aspect, voice

In modern linguistics, the word "tense" is used in the **morphological** sense, to designate an inflected form of a verb. Using this narrow definition, it follows that there are only two tenses in English, the present and the past.

However it is no less valid to take the word "tense" in its wider **semantic** (meaning-based) sense. This is the historic approach to English tenses, as used by Dr. Samuel Johnson, among others, who listed **six** English tenses, each of them with a simple and a progressive or continuous aspect.

While the narrow morphological definition of "tense" may be appropriate in terms of linguistic analysis, it can be very confusing for students and language learners. For this reason it is pedagogically preferable, and far clearer, to look on tenses as semantic categories, as is common practice in the world of EFL. / ESL.

Here is a table of the main tenses in English, in simple and progressive aspect, and active and passive voices: sample verb - to make.

Aspect voice Tense (form)	Simple active	Progressive active	Simple passive	Progressive passive
Present	I make	I am making	I am made	I am being made
Future with *will*	I will make	I will be making	I will be made	*rare*
Preterite	I made	I was making	I was made	I was being made
Present Perfect	I have made	I have been making	I have been made	*rare*
Past perfect	I had made	I had been making	I had been made	*rare*
Future perfect	I will have made	I will have been making	I will have been made	*rare*

▶ **Present tenses**: for examples, explanations and further details, see §1.2. below: the present tense.

▶ **The future**: for examples, explanations and further details, see § 1.3. below: expressing the future.

▶ **Past tenses**; for examples, explanations and further details on the different past tenses in English, including the "present perfect", see § 1.4. below: past tenses.

Rare forms:

Other "tenses" may exist in English for some verbs, in specific contexts; for example we could envisage *"It will be being repaired "* or *"He's been being looked after"*, but forms like this are very rare. Here, nonetheless, is a plausible example of a future progressive passive, which is quite acceptable in this particular case:

While you're on holiday in Majorca, **I'll be being interviewed** for that job in Glasgow.

1.1.4. Other verb forms in English: modality

Other forms or tenses, and notably conditionals, are formed with the help of modal verbs: can, could, may, might, would, plus must, should and ought to. These forms are structured in the same way as the future or future perfect. **These are the only structures possible using modal auxiliaries.**

Here is a table of modal verb forms, using the modal auxiliary *must*.

Modality *Aspect*	Modality in the present or future	Modality in the past
Simple, active	I must take	I must have taken
Progressive, active	I must be taking	I must have been taking
Simple, passive	I must be taken	I must have been taken
Progressive, passive	*rare*	*rare*

1.1.5. Moods

Verbs can be used in three different **moods**

- The indicative (§ 1.2 to § 1.5)
- The subjunctive (§ 1.1.6)
- The imperative (§ 1.7)

Most of the time, verbs are used in the **indicative** mood, which is the normal mood, as illustrated in all the examples above.

As a distinctive verb form, the **subjunctive** is very rare in English, and is normally found only in a few expressions, the most common of which is *If I were you*. See next section - § 1.1.6 below.

The **imperative** is used to give orders, instructions, invitations.

1.1.6. The subjunctive in English

Most English-speakers do not know that there is a subjunctive mood in English; but there is, and many use it quite regularly, without realising. However there is only one context in which the subjunctive is commonly used, and that is in the context of hypothetical conditional statements. And of these, there is just one recognisably subjunctive expression that is used - from time to time - by most people, and it is: *If I **were** you* as in:

> If I were you, I'd drive more carefully.

Note that the expression is "*If I were you*" (a subjunctive), and not "*If I was you*" (an indicative), though the second form is also heard.

With all verbs except *to be,* the **present subjunctive** is **identical** in form to the preterite, to the point that the existence of the present subjunctive as a tense in its own right is largely irrelevant in terms of modern grammar.

1.2. The present tenses in English

1.2.1. Different types of present tense in English

English uses **two** forms of the present, the **Present simple** and **the Present progressive.** This section looks at verbs in the active voice.

▶ For forms of the present tenses in the passive voice, see §1.8. The Passive.

1.2.2. The present simple

In short, the **Present Simple** is used to express:
  a) **permanent** states and permanent truths
  b) **repetitive** actions
  c) **instant** actions (present or future).

Examples – Present simple

> a1) I **like** apples, but I **don't like** oranges.
> a2) I **live** in London, and I **work** for a big bank.
> a3) Flowers **grow** well in a warm sunny climate.
> a4) Tomorrow never **comes**.
> b1) My brother often **goes** to London.
> b2) It **snows** in winter in New York.
> b3) I **get** up at 6 every morning.
> c1) Oh, I **understand** what you mean.
> c2) And now Messi **gets** the ball, he **shoots**, and he **scores**!
> c3) He **leaves** tomorrow.

1.2.2.1. The present simple affirmative

It is formed using the root form of the verb: there is only one ending to add, an **S** on the third person singular, or **ES** onto verbs ending in **-s, -sh, -x,** and **– o.**

Sample verbs	1st sing.	2nd sing.	3rd sing.	1st plural	2nd plural	3rd plural
Bring	I bring	you bring	he, she, it bring**s**	we bring	you bring	they bring
Do	I do	you do	he, she, it do**es**	we do	you do	they do
Pass	I pass	you pass	he, she, it pass**es**	we pass	you pass	they pass

1.2.2.2. The present simple negative

For all verbs, the present simple negative is formed using the root of the verb, and the auxiliary *do* in the negative form: **do not** and **does not** are normally contracted in spoken English, and may also be contracted in the written language.

Sample verbs	1st sing.	2nd sing.	3rd sing.	1st plural	2nd plural	3rd plural
Bring	I do not / don't bring	you do not / don't bring	he, she, it does not / do**es**n't bring	we do not / don't bring	you do not / don't bring	they do not / don't bring
Speak	I don't speak	you don't speak	he, she, it do**es**n't speak	we don't speak	you don't speak	they don't speak

1.2.3. The present progressive

In short, the **Present Progressive** is used to express:
 a) developing situations.
 b) actions that are actually taking place.
 c) **future** actions.

1.2.3.1. The present progressive affirmative

This is formed using the **present participle** of the verb and the present tense of **to be**. The present participle is formed by adding **-ing** to the root (or to the root minus its final *-e* for verbs ending in *e*). The auxiliary is usually contracted in spoken English (as in the second line of the sample verbs table below).

Examples – Present progressive

> a1) John **is getting** better.
> a2) The weather **isn't improving.**
> b1) This week I **am working** in New York.
> b2) Look! That man**'s stealing** my car!
> b3) Slow down, you**'re going** too fast!
> c1) He**'s not going** on holiday **tomorrow**.
> c2) He said he**'s retiring next year.**

Sample verbs	1st sing.	2nd sing.	3rd sing.	1st plural	2nd plural	3rd plural
Stand	I am standing	you are standing	he, she, it is standing	we are standing	you are standing	they are standing
Take	I'm taking	you're taking	he, she, it's taking	we're taking	you're taking	they're taking

1.2.3.2. The present progressive negative

The **negative** is formed by adding the particle *not*: there are two different ways of contracting the present progressive negative, as illustrated by the two lines of examples for the verb *take*. Contracted forms are normally preferred in spoken English, but may sometimes be used in the written language too, especially if the style is informal.

Sample verbs	1st sing.	2nd sing.	3rd sing.	1st plural	2nd plural	3rd plural
Stand	I am not standing	you are not standing	he, she, it is not standing	we are not standing	you are not standing	they are not standing
Take	I'm not taking	you're not taking	he, she, it's not taking	we're not taking	you're not taking	they're not taking
Take		you aren't taking	he, she, it isn't taking	we aren't taking	you aren't taking	they aren't taking

▶ See § 4.5. for more on **negation** in general.

Some verbs are never used in the progressive form

Take care ! Some verbs are almost never used in the present progressive - notably certain verbs of permanent state, such as **know, be, like, exist.**

We can say: *I know the train is arriving late*.
  We **cannot** say: *I **am knowing** the train is arriving late*.

1.2.4. Present simple vs. present progressive:

A contrastive example:

This sentence is a clear example of the difference in usage between the two forms:

> Yes I **eat** hamburgers, but **I'm not eating** a hamburger right now !

1.3. Expressing the future in English

1.3.1. Forms of the future in English

If you talk to a linguist, he or she may tell you that there is no such thing as the "*future tense*" as far as the English language is concerned! There are just two groups of tenses; those that refer to events in past time, and those that talk about the present or the future. But let's not split hairs; in semantic terms, English, like many other languages, has future tenses: indeed there are **three** ways of using a verb to express the future in English, and one of these is to use the present tense as a future tense.

1.3.2. The present tense used as a future tense

Very often, we use a present tense in English to talk about future events. Look at this short dialogue:

> "Where **are you going** next summer?"
> "We**'re staying** at home. I**'m working** all summer!"
> "Oh what a pity. **Don't** you even get a week off?"
> "Well perhaps; we **may go** to Wales for a couple of days."

Although this dialogue clearly refers to the **future**, the verbs are all in forms of the present. There is no **"will"**, no **"going to"**.

Present forms are the simplest way of expressing future time in many cases: the **present progressive** often expresses non-defined time in the future, the **present simple** refers to instant defined moments in time, or events that will occur regularly.

This does not mean that using a specific future tense would be wrong; we could rephrase the previous dialogue using the words **going to** (rather than will) to stress the future nature of events (remembering that going to is actually the present progressive tense of go.)

> "Where **are** you **going to go** this summer?"
> "We**'re going to stay** at home; I**'m going to work** all summer."
> "Oh what a pity. **Aren't** you even **going to get** a week off?"
> "Well perhaps; maybe **we'll go** to Wales ...."

But in most contexts, this would sound stilted or **heavy**.

1.3.3. The future with "will" or "going to"

A "future" with **will** is used to imply **predetermined actions** or **planned or programmed events**.

> "**Are you coming** home tonight, darling?"
> "Yes; my plane **gets** in at 8.15."
> "O.K. then, I**'ll meet** you at the airport."
>
> ---
>
> The President **will** arrive by plane at midday, then he**'ll** go straight to the conference.

It is also used to avoid confusion between present and future (e.g. when there is no adverb of time present). Compare: *I see / I'll see* or *I'm there / I'll be there.*

Note: the contraction *gonna* (for going to) is only used in spoken English.

1.3.3.1. *Cases* where **will/ going to** must or cannot be used.

a) *Will* and *going* to **cannot** be used with the modal verbs **can, could, must, should, would**. If it is essential to mark the future aspect of a modal structure, it is necessary to use **have to** instead of **must**, and **be able to** instead of **can**, as in: *You'll have to do better next time.*

One could also say: *You **must** do better next time.*

▶ See also: can, could, must, should

b) They are not used in **time clauses** after **if, when, as soon as, unless, after, before, while** etc, A "present tense" future is needed. On the other hand a future with **will** (or *going to*) **IS** required in the **main clause** if the action is in the future. Compare the verbs tenses in these examples.

> **We'll** have a picnic tomorrow **if it's** dry.
> **He'll** open the door **as soon as he hears** the bell.
> **I'll** tell you the rest of the story **when we get** home.

▶ See also: § 1.5. Conditional structures (if clauses).

c) **Take care !** Generally speaking, **will** is **not** used **in subordinate clauses** when **futurity** is marked by the verb the **main clause**. Except in some relative clauses, it is very unusual to find a future tense in both the main clause and a subordinate clause.

> **I'll sell** it to the first person who **makes** a good offer.
> They**'ll mend** it for you while you **wait**.
> You**'ll do** whatever you**'re told** to do!
> **I'll call you** as soon as I **land** in New York. (**not** will land.)

1.3.4. The future with shall

Shall and the negative form **shan't** are not often used in modern English; more than just expressing a future action, they express a future **obligation** or **certainty** (or in the negative, a **forbidding**), and are normally only used in the first person singular (with I), as in:

> I **shall** certainly visit the British Museum when I'm in London.
> I **shan't** be able to come next week, as I'm away on business.

But in both of these examples, **will / won't** are quite acceptable alternatives. **To avoid any risk of error,** the simplest principle to adopt is "*never say shall*". Don't use these forms! There is always an alternative.
▶ See also § 1.15: Modal verbs of obligation.

1.3.5. Negative forms of the future

These should not cause any problem for learners of English..
For negative forms of the present tense used with a future meaning, see § 1.2. The present tense.
- The negative forms of **will** are **won't** or **will not.**
- The negative forms of **going to** are **not going to**, with full or contracted forms of the auxiliary.
- The negative forms of **shall** are **shan't** or **shall not.**

> I **won't** be home for dinner tonight, darling.
> The guard **isn't going to** / is not going to open the doors until 9.
> I **shan't be able to** come next week, as I'm on holiday.

1.3.6. Other forms and tenses expressing the future

For **passive** forms of future tenses, see §1.8. The passive. For the future perfect tense (as in I will have seen), see below §1.4.5. The future perfect.

1.4. Past tenses in English

The currently popular view of modern linguistics argues that there is only one past tense in English, the "past". This can be very confusing for students, whether they are native speakers or learners of English. It is therefore more coherent to consider the idea of "tense" from the semantic or pragmatic viewpoint, which distinguishes **three past tenses** in English - the **simple past** (or preterite), the **present perfect**, and the **past perfect** (or pluperfect).

The three past tenses of English all have simple and progressive forms, as illustrated below. These tenses can be used in the active or the passive.

1.4.1. Forms of past tenses: sample verb make

1. **Simple active** forms

	I	you	he she it one	we	you	they
Simple past	made						
Present perfect	have made	has made			have made		
Past perfect	had made					

2. **Progressive active** forms

	I	you	he she it one	we	you	they
Simple past	was making	were making				
Present perfect	have been making		has been making	have been making		
Past perfect	had been making					

For **passive** forms, ▶ see § 1.8 The Passive.

1.4.2. The simple past (or preterite)

This is used to relate past events in a **historic context.** Often, you will know that it must be used, because the sentence also contains an adverb (or adverb phrase) of time, such as *yesterday*, or a date or time or a time clause like "*when I was younger*".

Examples

1. Queen Victoria **died** *in 1901.*
2. The Titanic **sank** *when it hit an iceberg.*
3. I **told** you not to drink too much.
4. *Next*, they **went** and **cooked** dinner.
5. I **liked** that kind of music *when I was younger.*

1.4.2.1. Simple past - progressive or continuous forms:

Here are some examples with a progressive or continuous form too: both of the events in each sentence are "historic", but one took place while another longer-lasting situation was true:

Examples

1. I first **met** my husband when I *was living* in New York.
2. The students **shouted** as the President *was speaking*.

1.4.2.2. Used to and would

The past of finished habit or terminated situation

To express a **finished habit**, there are two additional possible structures, one with **used to**, the other with **would**.

To express a **terminated situation**, only the structure with **used to** can be used. Terminated situation can also be expressed using the simple past often reinforced by an adverb of duration or of time.

Examples

1. I **used to go** to Brighton when I was a child (but I don't any longer.)
2. He **would call** her every day when she was younger (but he doesn't now.)
3. This street **used to be** full of traffic; but now it's very quiet.
4. This street **was once** full of traffic; but now it's very quiet

1.4.3. The Present Perfect (or compound past)

In British English, the **present perfect** (which Samuel Johnson called quite appropriately, the *compound preterite*) is used to situate past events, or the consequences of past events, **in relation to the present situation** (that's why it is known as the "present" perfect). American English speakers do not always use the present perfect in this situation.

Examples

1. I **have ordered** a new refrigerator, darling!
   (i.e., the speaker means "*A new refrigerator is coming and will be here soon*").
2. **I've eaten** too much!
   (i.e. the speaker implies: "*At this moment now, I do not feel very well; I have a funny feeling in my stomach!*)
3. Manchester United **have won** the Cup.
   (i.e. *Manchester United are now, at this moment , football champions*).
4. He's **broken** his leg, so he can't play football this week.

You do not usually find **adverbs of time** used with verbs in the present perfect, but there are some **exceptions**:

   1. already:
   2. adverbs of frequency:
   3. adverbs or adverb phrases of duration related to the present:

Examples

1. Come on, *we've **already started*** eating !
2. **I've often seen** people driving too fast down that road.
3. **I've lived** in London **for ten years.**
   (**Contrast with:** *I lived in London for ten years* (but I don't live there now -- a historic statement)
4. **I've lived** in London **since 2005.**
5. **I've been living** in London **since 2005.**   (*Both of these forms are acceptable*)
6. Up to now, **I've always refused** to eat fish.

1.4.3.1. Present-perfect progressive or present-perfect continuous:

These progressive forms are used when we want to imply that an event / events in the past have been continuing until the present point in time, or have taken place over a period of time in the past.

I've been waiting for you since three o'clock.
The doctor **has been seeing** patients for most of the afternoon.

(▶ See § 3.2.2. for more on: *since and for*)

1.4.4. The past perfect or pluperfect.

The past perfect or pluperfect, as in *He had seen*, is normally only used in English when one past event (either a specific action, or a continuous condition) has to be situated *in a more distant past* than another past event. In some situations, the progressive or continuous form is necessary.

Examples

I **had just put** the phone down, when the doorbell rang.
The man **had been drinking** before the accident happened.
He **had worked** in the company for five years before he got promotion.

There are some other uses too, but they are less common. Note, for example, the use of the past perfect (and inversion) after **hardly**:

Hardly **had** I **put** the phone down, than the phone rang.

1.4.5. The future perfect

The future perfect, as in **He will have seen,** is a form that is not common, but is sometimes useful in order to relate two future events or points in time, one of which will be in the past *before* the other takes place or is true. It can be used in simple or progressive forms, as in these clear examples.

I **will have finished** reading the report before midnight. *(future perfect simple)*
He **won't have been climbing** for long before he reaches the really difficult part. *(future perfect progressive)*

1.5. The Conditional in English

Conditional clauses in English, after if or unless

1.5.1. Definition of a conditional clause

A conditional clause is a type of subordinate clause, most commonly introduced by the conjunction *if* or *unless*, or occasionally *whether*. Like most subordinate clauses introduced by a conjunction, the conditional clause can either go **before** the main clause, or **after** it.

There are three types of conditional statement in English:

1. **Type 1**: Open conditional *as in* If you want, you can go home.
2. **Type 2**: Hypothetical conditional *as in* If you wanted, you could go home.
3. **Type 3**: Unfulfilled hypothetical *as in* If you had wanted, you could have gone home.
4. (Hypothetical conditional clauses can also be formed **without if**).

1.5.2. Open *if* clause - the open conditional statement

Open conditional (Type 1) *if* clauses are most commonly used to speak of one event or situation which is conditional on another .

Type 1a. One future event is dependent on another. The verb of the **main** clause is in the **future tense** with "*will*" (or sometimes another modal). The verb of the **conditional** clause is in the **simple present** tense.

Type 1b. One potentially constant state of reality or circumstance is dependent on another. In this case **both verbs** are in the **present** tense.

Type 1c. If the time-frame in the past, both verbs are normally in the simple **preterite**, though sometimes the verb in the conditional clause may be in the past progressive.

1a If you **have** a coffee at night, you **won't sleep** well.
1a If you **finish** in the first ten, you**'ll get** a medal.
1b If I **sleep** well at night, I **feel** much happier next morning.
1b If the temperature **falls** below zero, it **freezes**.
1b If it **rains**, everyone **gets** wet.
1c If I **slept** well at night, I **felt** much happier next morning.
1c If it **rained**, everybody **got** wet.
1c Nobody **listened** if he was shouting too much

In an open conditional statement, **if** is sometimes replaced by **when**: but there is a difference. Using "**if**" implies that the condition really is open and may not be fulfilled, using "**when**" implies that the condition will / would be fulfilled, that the event will / would really take place.

1.5.3. Open hypothetical conditional statement

We use an open hypothetical conditional (Type 2) if clause to refer to a possible future situation which depends on an another possible future situation.

The verb of the **main clause** uses the **present conditional** tense (*would* + infinitive, or *could* +infinitive);

The verb of the **conditional clause** normally uses the **present subjunctive** or **preterite** (these two tenses are identical except with *to be*). Occasionally, the conditional aspect of the statement can be emphasised by using the form *were + to* + infinitive.

1A	If you **ate** too much, **you'd (you** would) **get** fatter.
1B	You**'d get** fatter if you **ate** too much.
2A	If everyone **worked** faster, we **would / could finish** in time.
2B	We **wouldn't finish** in time unless everyone **worked** faster.
2C	If everyone **were to work** faster, we **would/could finish** in time.
3	If I **went** to London, I **would / could visit** the British Museum.
4.	If you **visited** Scotland, you **could see** Edinburgh Castle.
5	Unless the directors **increased** sales, **we'd have to** close this shop.

Note also this common expression (which uses the open hypothetical form, though it is clearly quite impossible!)

6. *If I were you, I'd ....* as in.
   If I **were** you, I'd go a bit slower
   If I **were** you, I'd put that gun down!!

Open hypothetical structures are also used in cases of **reported or indirect speech**, when reporting an original statement using a type 1 conditional sentence

My professor told me **I'd do** much better *if I worked harder.*
   (Original statement: "*You'll do much better if you **work** harder.*")
The magistrate informed him that **he'd go** to prison *unless he stopped stealing.*
   (Original statement: "You'll go to prison unless you **stop** stealing")
The newspaper reported that *unless the directors could increase sales,* **they'd have to close** the shop.

1.5.4. The unfulfilled hypothesis

This refers to a situation in which an event **might have** taken place, but did **not**, because a condition was <u>not</u> fulfilled.

The verb of the **main** clause goes in the **past conditional** (*would / could* etc. + *have* + past participle).

The verb of the **conditional** clause is in the **past perfect** (*had* + past participle).

> If you **had eaten** too much, you'**d** (you **would**) **have got** fatter.
> You'd have got fatter if you'**d eaten** too much.
> If everyone **had worked** fast, we'**d have finished** in time (*but we didn't*).
> We **wouldn't / couldn't / mightn't** etc. **have finished** in time unless everyone **had worked** fast (*but we did*).
> If I **had gone** to London, I **could have visited** the British Museum (*but I didn't*).
> If you **had visited** Scotland, you **could have visited** Edinburgh Castle (*but you didn't*).
> Unless we'**d been** very confident of success, we **wouldn't have even tried.** (*But we were confident, we did try, and we succeeded*).

Note: using " *unless*"

"Unless" means the same as "**if ... not**", and has a negative value. It is frequently (but not only) used in conditional statements where the verb of the main clause is also in the negative.

> You *wouldn't have fallen* over **unless** *there'd been* a banana skin on the ground.
> = You **wouldn't have fallen** over **if** there **hadn't been** a banana skin on the ground.

1.5.5. Omission of "if", with inversion

Sometimes, **hypothetical conditional statements** or **unfulfilled hypothetical statements** can be expressed **omitting** the word *if*. When this happens the **subject** follows the **auxiliary verb** in the conditional clause.

> **Were the virus** to reappear, hospitals would now be ready for it. (open hypothesis).
> = If the virus reappeared, hospitals would now be ready for it. *or* If the virus were to reappear, hospitals would now be ready for it.
> **Had I** known, I'd never have gone there (unfulfilled hypothesis; implying "*I did go there because I did not know*".)
> = If I had known, I'd never have gone there.

1.5.6. Whether

Whether is often used in place of **if**, when there is a stated or implied **choice** of conditions. **Whether** is generally required before **or not**.

> I'll stop at midday **whether** I've finished by then **or not**.
> I wonder **whether / if** it will rain tomorrow **(or not)**.

For more about **whether**, see §3.3.3. Correlating coordinators.

1.6. The infinitive in English

The **active present infinitive** - normally known as just "the infinitive" - is the basic or root form of a verb. In English, it can take two forms, with or without the particle *to*. For example:

> **live** or **to live**, **love** or **to love**, **think** or **to think**.

There is also a past infinitive, as in *to have loved*.
▶ See also: § 1.10. Consecutive verbs: gerund or infinitive?

Occasionally infinitives are used in a **progressive** form, as in *to be thinking*

Use of the infinitive

An infinitive cannot be used as the main verb of a sentence: it can only be used in a subordinate infinitive phrase or infinitive clause. Even Shakespeare's most famous expression, "**To be, or not to be?**" is really a subordinate clause. The full sentence is "*To be, or not to be; that is the question.*" or in other words: *"The question is whether to be or not to be"*.

1.6.1. The short infinitive, without *to*

This is the **exception**. It is used notably with certain modal auxiliaries, **can, could, may, might, will, shall, could, must.**

> The manager will **need** a holiday.
> When I was younger, I couldn't **read** very well.
> You must **put** on a coat, it's cold outside.
> She should **be thinking** of her children.

It is also found after a few other verbs that introduce a verb complement, in particular: *dare*, verbs of primary perception *see, hear, smell, feel,* and some verbs of permission or causative verbs, notably *make, let* and *have*. Finally there are two common words that are followed by a short infinitive: these are rather and better, in expressions on the model *I'd rather....*

I dare **say** you've never met my brother James.
I heard him **leave** the office by the back door.
I felt her **touch** me very gently on the arm.
I can't make this car **start**.
I'm free!! They let me **go**!
The teacher had the class **redo** the test because he had lost the papers.
You'd better **clean** the kitchen before your mum gets home.
I'd rather **be spending** my holidays at the seaside.

After verbs of perception, the second verb can alternatively be a **present participle**:

I heard him **leave** the house by the front door. *Or*
I heard him **leaving** the house by the front door.

Both these structures are possible, though there may be a shade of difference in meaning between the two; normally the speaker can choose.

1.6.2. The full infinitive, with *to*

The infinitive as verbal complement.

This is the most common use of the infinitive. The infinitive is found in many verbal complements, and notably after the following verbs (among others):

want, wish, have, ought, like, need, hope, expect, fail, pretend, refuse, demand, apply, agree, try.

Examples

I **wish to leave**, and I would **like to go** home.
You **need to see** a doctor as soon as possible.
He **asked to see** the manager, so I **agreed to** let him in.
I fully **expect to finish/ to be finishing** the job tomorrow.
I **want** you **to tell** me the whole story.
I'm afraid that **I fail to understand** what you are trying to say.

1.6.3. Past infinitives

1.6.3.1. The past infinitive, active.

This is formed using the full present infinitive of the auxiliary *have*, with the past participle of the verb. For example: *to have eaten, to have lost*. Its use is identical to that of the present infinitive. The **short form** of the past infinitive, without *to*, is only used after modal verbs such as *may, would*. (▶ see § 1 15. Modal verbs). Occasionally the past infinitive is used in a **progressive** form , as in *to have been eating.*

Examples

I want **to have finished** the job, before I go home
You need **to have passed** the test, or else you won't be admitted.
Uh! You're supposed **to have been painting** it blue, not pink!
I'd like **to have seen** his expression, when he opened the letter!
At last! The rain seems **to have stopped** !
I **may have told** you before, I really can't remember.
Help! I **must have left** my passport in the hotel.
Oh dear! I **must have been sitting** on a strawberry.

1.6.4. Passive infinitives

These are formed using the full present or past infinitive of the auxiliary *be* with the past participle of the verb. For example: *to be eaten, to have been eaten, to be found, to have been found.* Their use is identical to those of active infinitives. The **short form** of the passive infinitive, without *to*, is only used after modal verbs such as *may, would.*

Examples

The car needs **to be cleaned** before you try to sell it.
The car needs **to have been cleaned** before you try to sell it.
The mayor likes **to be invited** to official dinners.
The door appears **to have been left** open all night.
He seems **to have been given** a very good mark.
You would **be given** a good mark, if you worked harder.
I'm sorry, I may **have been recognised**.
They are very lucky, they could **have been killed**.

1.6.5. Infinitive or gerund?

(▶See also § 1.10: Consecutive verbs: gerund or infinitive.) A few verbs, such as *try, love, prefer, or start* can take a verbal complement either in the form of an infinitive, or as a gerund, with little or no change of meaning. But to avoid a repetition of *-ing*, it is preferable to put the second verb in the infinitive if the first verb is in a progressive form.

1.6.6. Other points

Take care ! Two verbs, *remember* and *stop* have different meanings depending on whether the following verb is in the infinitive or is a gerund. As for *forget*, it is normally followed by an infinitive, rarely by a gerund.

> I stopped **to listen** to the music .
> = *I stopped something else in order to listen to the music.*
> I stopped **listening** to the music = *I finished listening to the music.*
> I remembered **to do** the shopping
> = *I did the shopping because I remembered.*
> I remember **doing** the shopping = *I know that I did the shopping.*
> I forgot **to buy** some milk on my way home.
> I forgot (about) **buying** milk on the way home.

1.6.6.1 *The infinitive as complement to an adjective.*

The infinitive with *to* is found as the complement of certain adjectives, following a comparative adjective, or after adjectives or adverbs qualified by an **adverb of degree** (*too, enough, so*, etc.).

Examples

> I was pleased **to see** you.
> It was very clever of you **to win** the prize.
> You'd do better* **to choose** a different holiday altogether.
> It's easier **to break** it than **to take** it apart.
> The offer really was **too** good **to be** true.
> It was **quite** hard **to know** who to believe.
> It was **so** good of you **to come** quickly.
> We got out of the building quickly **enough to avoid** being seen.
> It wasn't **all that** easy **to understand.**

Note: Do not confuse: *You'd better* finish.... with *You'd do better to* finish

1.6.6.2. *Other uses of the infinitive with to:*

The infinitive with *to* is also found as an abbreviation of the form *in order to* + verb:

> I went home **to get** some sleep. *or*
> I went home **in order to get** some sleep.

Just occasionally, but with a slight change of meaning, it can be found, like a gerund, as the subject of a sentence.

> **To win** the big contract would be a great success.

or to quote some famous lines from Shakespeare in *Hamlet* and Oscar Wilde in *the Importance of being Earnest:*

> **To be or not to be,** that is the question.
> **To lose** one parent, Mr Worthing, may be regarded as a misfortune; **to lose** both looks like carelessness.

But these examples use a rather formal and old-fashioned style

1.6.6.3. The infinitive in indirect questions:

The infinitive can also be used in some indirect questions using a question word such as *what, where, how* etc. when - in the indirect question - the main clause and the indirect question clause have the same subject.

> "**How can I get to Chicago?**"
> ▶ He asked me how he could get to Chicago,
>   or: He asked me how to get to Chicago.
> "**What do we see next?**"
> ▶ They asked what they should see next,
>   or: They asked what to see next.

1.6.7. Split infinitives

There is a persistent rumour that it is not acceptable to split infinitives in English. This is absolutely wrong. Infinitives can be split, and have always been able to be split in good English. Indeed, there are cases in which it is virtually **essential** to split infinitives, unless you want to resort to a long and cumbersome paraphrase.

The most famous split infinitive of modern times is the classic introduction to the **Star Trek** TV series, which went:

> These are the voyages of the Starship Enterprise, its 5 year mission to explore strange new worlds, to seek out new life and new civilizations, **to boldly go** where no man has gone before.

In this case the split infinitive is not essential; the text could have said *"to go boldly",* so in this case there is no compelling reason to use a split infinitive. In other cases, there is. Look at this example.

> The doctors decided **to rapidly stop** administering pain-killers.

It is not possible to put the word *rapidly* anywhere else in the sentence without either making it **ambiguous**, or else **changing the meaning**. Compare these examples.

> The doctors decided **to rapidly stop** administering pain-killers.
> **Rapidly** the doctors decided to stop administering pain-killers.
> The doctors decided **rapidly** to stop administering pain-killers.
> The doctors decided to stop **rapidly** administering pain-killers.
> The doctors decided to stop administering pain-killers **rapidly**.

The only way in this example to avoid the split infinitive while not changing the meaning is to write a longer periphrase:

The doctors decided they would rapidly stop administering the pain killers.

Great writers and split infinitives

Until the twentieth century, even more so than today, split infinitives were uncommon; but great writers used them from time to time.

> "They had indeed some boats in the river, but they ... served **to just waft** them over, or to fish in them." *Daniel Defoe*
> "Milton was too busy **to much miss** his wife." *Samuel Johnson*

From the 19th century onwards, writers resorted more and more often to using split infinitives; Abraham Lincoln used them, so did Wordsworth, Henry James and Robert Burns – and many more too.

Why do some people object to split infinitives?

The reasons are historical, and invented. The first attempts to describe English grammar reflected principles of Latin grammar, and in Latin as in Greek, splitting an infinitive really is impossible, since the infinitive is a single word (as in *amare* or *legere*). So to make "good" English like Latin, early grammarians decided that the infinitive was something that should not be split. There is no other reason.

In the nineteenth century, traditional grammars continued to claim that splitting infinitives was bad grammar; but writers were using them more and more. Since the early twentieth century, it has become more or less accepted that split infinitives are not just acceptable, but in some cases unavoidable. And why not? An infinitive is a verb form, and in English most verb forms contain two words which can, and in some cases must, be split.

1.7. The imperative in English

1.7.1. Uses of the imperative

The imperative forms of verbs are used for several specific but similar purposes:
- **To give orders or instruct**
- **To warn**
- **To encourage**
- **To invite**

1.7.2. Forms of the imperative

Imperatives are most commonly used in the active and in the **second person**, i.e. implying **you**. The pronoun is however omitted. They are occasionally used in the first and third persons, with the help of the auxiliary *let*. In all cases, the verb or the auxiliary stands at the start of the sentence.

Sample verb: Look	Affirmative	Negative
Common imperative: second person (you)	*Look*	*Don't look*
First person (I, we)	*Let me look* / *Let's wait*	*Don't let me look* / *Let's not wait*
Third person (he, she, it, they etc.)	*Let him look (etc.)*	*Don't let him look (etc.)*

Examples: simple imperatives - second person

> **Tell** him to go home.
> **Shut** up!
> **Give** me your answer by Friday!
> **Don't let** any of the prisoners escape.
> **Don't pretend** you never saw anyone enter the house!
> **Make** sure no-one sees you!
> **Come** for dinner tomorrow evening!
> **Don't hesitate** to ask if you need help.

Imperatives and style.

The imperative form by itself can be rather blunt, rather abrupt, even rude. It can be made less abrupt, more polite, by the addition of **softeners** such as *please, would you please*, etc.

Examples: soft imperatives

> **Please tell** him to go home.
> **Would you shut** up!
> **Would you give** me your answer by Friday, please!
> **Please don't let** any of the prisoners escape.
> **Please don't pretend** you never saw anyone enter the house!

First and third person imperatives are not common, but there are some common expressions that use them.

> **Let** me **see**!
> **Let's go.**
> **Let's** not **wait** any longer.
> **Let** him **think** what he wants!

Passive imperatives

These are rare: here are a couple of examples:

> **Don't be taken** by surprise!   **Let** them **not be** forgotten.

1.7.3. Emphatic imperatives

There are two ways of adding emphasis to an imperative.
- Occasionally the pronoun **you** is added to simple imperatives, in order to add emphasis or to specify to whom the imperative is addressed. See examples 1 - 4
- Alternatively **do** can be added at the start of the sentence, as a redundant auxiliary. See examples 5 - 7

Examples

1. *You* wait until your turn!
2. Shut up, *you*!
3. *You* wait here while I go for assistance!
4. *You* watch the front door, and you watch the back!
5. *Do* have another cup of tea, if you'd like to.
6. *Do* put that gun down please, you're frightening people!
7. Oh *do* shut up!

The examples with added **you** may not look like emphatic imperatives, but they are. The **you**s can be omitted, and the meaning remains the same. They are thus optional, not required as in an indicative context.

1.8. Voices – active and passive

1.8.1. Usage

In European languages, including English, verbs can be used in two different "voices", called the **active** and the **passive.** The active voice is by far the more common of the two. Here are some simple examples of verbs used in the active voice.

Box A: Examples – sentences expressed in the active voice.

1. I **love** football.
2. The people **were talking** very loudly.
3. Winston Churchill **wrote** reports every day.
4. James **hit** the ball very hard.

Most sentences can be expressed without any need to use forms of the passive; however sometimes we may want to change the way a sentence is expressed, in order to imply a slightly different meaning. Generally speaking, it is only **transitive** sentences (sentences that have a direct object) that can be rephrased in the passive.

So let's look at the same four examples again, re-expressed using a passive verb, *when this is possible*.

Box B: the same sentences expressed in the passive.

1. **No!** Football **is loved** by me..... *This sounds very strange! It would never be said, even if it is technically possible.*
2. **No!** This sentence cannot be rephrased in the pass*ive*.. **Talk** *is an intransitive verb.*
3. **OK.** Reports **were written** every day by Winston Churchill.
4. **OK.** The ball **was hit** very hard by James.

The **passive** is used, essentially, in three situations:

- To put more **emphasis** on the word that would be the object of an active sentence.
- To write an **impersonal** sentence.
- To simplify the **structure** of a complex sentence.

Let's see examples of these three situations.

1.8.2. Using the passive for emphasis

Now let's compare sentences 3 and 4 from boxes A and B above.

3a.	Winston Churchill **wrote** reports every day.
3b.	Reports **were written** every day by Winston Churchill.
4a.	James **hit** the ball very hard.
4b.	The ball **was hit** very hard by James.

Sentences 3a and 4a describe human actions – which is what most everyday sentences do.

Sentences 3b and 4b describe the same actions, but place **objects** (*reports / ball*) at the centre of the action, by making them into the subject of passive sentences.

In these normal "passive transformations" the **direct object** of the active sentence becomes the **subject** of the passive sentence.

Occasionally however, instead of the direct object, it is the **indirect** object of an active sentence that can become the subject of a passive sentence. ▶ See § 1.8.5. the Passive followed by an object, below.

1.8.3. Using the passive to make an impersonal sentence

In this case, the passive is used as a tool of formal **style** (see § 4.9. styles) to express actions that are not specifically linked to any person. We can thus remove the person from sentences 3b and 4b, which then become non-personal, and rather **formal**.

3c. Reports **were written** every day.
4c. The ball **was hit** very hard.

Here are three more examples of formal non-personal use of the passive.

5. The students **were told** to assemble at 9.30 a.m.
6. A public meeting **will be held** in the Town Hall next Friday.
7. It**'s reported** that the Prime Minister has at last resigned.

In these examples, the writer does not tell us – maybe does not want to tell us – who has told the students to assemble, nor who is organising a public meeting, nor who says that the PM is going to resign. Either it is not important, or the writer prefers not to say, or maybe the writer is not sure if it is actually true.

1.8.4. Using the passive to simplify sentence structure

Often, meaning is easier to understand if we use the **same subject** for a sequence of sentences or clauses: sometimes, this may require the use of a passive structure for one or more of the clauses.

Examples - using a passive to simplify a sequence of clauses.

> 1a. I arrived in London. My brother met me at the station.
> 1b. I arrived in London and was met by my brother at the station.
> 2a. The guests were waiting for an hour before someone gave them a drink.
> 2b. The guests were waiting for an hour before they were given a drink.

1.8.5. Forms of the passive

Most of the active forms of transitive verbs, including the infinitive and the imperative, have equivalent forms in the passive. But **intransitive verbs** cannot be used in the passive.

Here is a table of examples for the verb to help.

Form / Tense *Aspect, voice*	Simple, active	Progressive, active	Simple, passive	Progressive, passive
Present	I help	I am helping	I am helped	I am being helped
Future	I will help	I will be helping	I will be helped	*rare*
Preterite	I helped	I was helping	I was helped	I was being helped
Present Perfect	I have helped	I have been helping	I have been helped	*rare*
Past perfect	I had helped	I had been helping	I had been helped	*rare*
Future perfect	I will have helped	I will have been helping	I will have been helped	*rare*

For more details see pages on the Present (§ 1.2.), the Past (§ 1.4.), and the Future(§ 1.3.). The passive can also sometimes be formed using the verb **get**, instead of **be**, as an auxiliary. (▶ See § 1.14 Get and got).

1.8.6. The passive followed by an object

Unlike in some other European languages, passive verb forms in English can sometimes be followed by a **direct object.** This is only possible when the **indirect object** of an active sentence becomes the subject of the passive sentence.

This happens with a **limited number of verbs**, known as "ditransitive verbs" among the most common of which are *give, tell, bring, teach, ask, pay, sell, send*,

Active sentences	Passive equivalent
The doctor gave **me** some medicine	I was given **some medicine** by the doctor.
Laura told **the children** a story.	**The children** were told **a story** by Laura.
They brought **the lady** a Christmas card	**The lady** was brought **a Christmas card.**
Mr. Potter taught **me** English	I was taught **English** by Mr. Potter.
The tourists asked **me** a question.	I was asked **a question** by the tourists.
My sister made **me** a chocolate cake.	I was made **a chocolate cake** by my sister.
The company paid **£200** to each man.	**Each man** was paid **£200** by the company.
The mayor sent **a letter** to the **residents.**	**The residents** were sent **a letter** by the mayor.

1.9. Gerunds and -ing words

Gerunds, verbal nouns or present participles ending in -ing

▶ See also § 1.10: Consecutive verbs.

1.9.1. The different types of word ending in -ing:

The English language does not use many grammatical "endings", but some of those it does use have several different functions. The *-ing* ending is one of them. Words ending in *-ing* can be gerunds, verbal nouns, or present participles. **Distinguishing** (= *gerund*) between these, and using them correctly is not always easy – until you understand these three simple rules.

Definitions

The gerund is a verb which is used as if it were a noun (Examples 1 & 2 below). Since it is a verb, it can **not** be qualified by an adjective, nor preceded by an article, but, like other forms of the verb, it can be modified by an adverb and take a complement.

A **verbal noun** (Examples 3 & 4) is a **noun** formed from a verb; some verbal nouns end in **-ing**.
Verbal nouns, like other nouns, <u>can</u> take a determiner, and be qualified by adjectives.

A **participle** is an adjective or part of a participial phrase qualifying a noun or a pronoun. (Examples 5 et 6). The present participle is also used in the **progressive** aspect of verb tenses (Examples 7 & 8).

See the differences of use that are illustrated by these examples.

Words in -ing: Gerund, noun or present participle (and progressive verb form)

1. **Seeing** is **believing**.
2. **Living** cheaply in New York is quite possible.
3. The book was easy **reading**!
4. He managed to make a good **living**.
5. **Smiling**, the lady told them they'd won the big prize.
6. I heard them **arguing** last night.
7. I'm **taking** my brother to the station tonight
8. The man was **phoning** his friend, when the lights went out.

1.9.2. The gerund in English: a verb used as a noun

The **gerund** in English has the form of the present participle in *-ing*.
It is the most common form of the verb used as a noun, and can be the subject (examples 1 to 7 below), or the object of a sentence (8 & 9, 14 to 16) , or follow prepositions (10 to 13).

Examples of gerunds

1. **Seeing** is believing.
2. **Reading** that book was very interesting.
3. **Drinking** is essential.
4. **Drinking** too much pop can make you fat.
5. **Taking** the bus was rather a good idea.
6. **Swimming** is very good exercise.
7. **Taking** too many aspirins is dangerous.
8. I really like **sailing**.
9. This article needs fully **rewriting**.
10. He drove two hundred miles without ever **stopping**.
11. I look forward to **seeing** you again next week.
12. I'm thinking of **painting** my house.
13. I started by carefully **turning** off the electricity.
14. Do you mind **shutting** the window, please?
15. Will you consider **taking** the job?
16. I've really enjoyed **meeting** you.

As the examples above show, the gerund is a verb used <u>as if it were</u> a noun, but <u>**not in the same way as**</u> a noun. In other words, **it keeps its verbal qualities.** Since it **is not a noun**, it cannot be qualified by an adjective; on the contrary, it keeps some of the essential features that distinguish a verb, notably that it can take a direct object (examples 2, 4, 7, 11 - 16 above) , and/or be qualified by an adverb (examples 6, 9 & 13).

When gerunds are used as **verbal complements** (second verbs following a first verb), as in examples 8 and 9 above, they can often be rephrased using an infinitive instead of the gerund (For example: *"This article needs to be fully rewritten"..* using a passive infinitive).

However a few verbs require a gerund, not an infinitive (Examples 14 - 16 above). The most common of these are *admit, consider, dislike, deny, enjoy, finish, involve, miss, mind, suggest,*

▶ For more details on this, see Annex 1. Consecutive verb structures at the end of this book.

1.9.3. Verbal nouns: nouns that are derived from verbs

There are a large number of ways of creating a noun from a verb: among the most common of these are words that use the root form of the verb and a noun ending such as **-ment** (as in *achievement*), **-ance** (as in *disappearance*), **-ion** (as in *confirmation*) , or **-ing** (as in *The changing of the guard*.) You can see that these -ing forms really are **nouns**, not verbs, as they can be qualified by adjectives

***Examples of** verbal nouns:*

1. That is a very nice **painting**.
2. We're going to see the **changing** of the guard at Buckingham Palace.
3. After a slow **beginning**, the show got a bit more lively.
4. This story has a rather unexpected **ending**.
5. The commission demanded the **breaking** up of the company into two separate units.
6. The last **meeting** was not very productive.

1.9.4. Areas of possible confusion

Sometimes it is difficult to decide if a word is a gerund or a verbal noun; and in fact, the quality of the **-ing** word can change *according to context*. Look at these examples:

Examples

1. For musicians, **practising** is essential.
2. For musicians, **practising** an instrument is essential
3. For musicians, regular **practising** is essential.
4. No ~~For musicians, regular practising an instrument is essential~~.
5. For musicians, **regularly** practising an instrument is essential.
6. For musicians, the regular **practising** of an instrument is essential.

In examples **1** and **2** above, *practising* is clearly a **gerund**; in example 2 it is followed by a complement, *an instrument*.

But in example **3** it is preceded by an adjective *regular*, so this time it is being used differently, as a **verbal noun**.

We can verify this if we try to add a complement, as in example **4**. **It is not possible.** We cannot say "~~For musicians, regular practising an instrument is essential.~~". **An *-ing* word cannot simultaneously be preceded by an**

adjective and followed by a direct complement. Other solutions are needed; the *ing* word must **either** be used as a gerund, **or** as a verbal noun, but **not both at once**.

So while example **4** does not work, there are two solutions.
   Example **5** uses the word *practising* as a gerund, as in examples 1 and 2; and being a gerund, it is modified by an adverb, *regularly*.
   Finally, example **6** rephrases example 5, but using *practising* as a **verbal noun**, not a gerund. We can see that it is a **noun**, as it is now part of a noun phrase introduced by an article and including an adjective.

1.9.5. Present participles

Participles are adjectives; they can either stand alone, before or after their noun, as the situation requires, or else they can be part of an adjectival phrase.

Participles are often used to make a shortened form of a subordinate clause, as in examples 1 and 3 below,

> In example 1 below, *Looking* out of... is an ellipsis or contraction of *As I was looking out of...*, and ...
> *I saw the tornado coming* is a contraction of ...*I saw the tornado that was coming*.

Elliptical phrases may come before the noun or pronoun (e.g. *Looking* out of the window, I saw ....) or after it (e.g. *I saw the tornado coming*).

   However, when the participle phrase is a shortened form of a relative clause, it **MUST** come after the noun (examples 4 & 7 below).

   Present participles are also used to form the progressive forms of present and past tenses as in Examples 8 – 10 below:

Examples of present *participles*:

1. **Looking** out of the window, I saw the tornado **coming**.
2. In the course of the **coming** week, I have three interviews to go to.
3. I saw the child **standing** in the middle of the road.
4. The people **living** next door are very friendly.
   - **No** 4b ~~The living next door people are very friendly~~ is impossible.
5. This is a seriously **interesting** book.
6. The **winning** team will go through to the finals.
7. The team **winning** in the first round will go through to the finals.
8. I was **looking** out of the window when I saw the tornado
9. At the moment, he's **living** in Bristol.
10. The company has been **doing** very well for the past two years.

1.9.6. -ing forms in passive structures

Gerunds and participles are most commonly used in the active voice; they can however be easily used in the passive too.

Examples 1 - 4 are **gerunds**, **examples 5 & 6** are **participles**.

Examples

1. **Being seen** is more important than **being heard**.
2. He drove two hundred miles without ever **being stopped**.
3. They began their holiday by **getting** hopelessly **lost**.
4. The town was evacuated after **having been** largely **destroyed**.
5. Everyone watched the building **getting demolished**.
6. At the moment they're **being sold** at half price.

1.10. Consecutive verbs in English

When to use an -ing form, and when to use an infinitive

> **Definitions**
> **Consecutive** verbs, also called **catenative verbs** or **linked verbs**, are verbs that can be followed <u>directly</u> by a second verb, the second verb being normally the **object** of the first.
>   Depending on the first verb used, the second verb will be in the form of a gerund (see § 1.9.2.) or of an infinitive with *to* (see § 1.6.2.). With a few verbs, there is a choice of structures; with most there is no choice.

While the definition of consecutive verbs applies also to auxiliaries and modal verbs, these are used differently, so are best considered as separate categories. These are treated on their own pages: See ▶ be, have, get and modal auxiliaries of obligation or possibility.

1.10.1. Gerund or infinitive? The main principles

Many learners of English have difficulty knowing whether the second verb in a linked verb pair should be a gerund in *-ing*, or an infinitive with **to**. As these common examples show, different verbs use different structures. For a full list of main consecutive verbs, see Appendix 1 at the end of this book.

Examples

> I **want to learn** English fast! *(with want a full infinitive is needed)*
> I **keep getting** confused by this question! *(with keep a gerund is needed)* .
> I **love meeting** my friends in the café after work!
> I **love to meet** my friends in the café after work! *(with love either a gerund or a full infinitive can be used).*

Confused? That's understandable! But luckily there are a couple of general principles that will help you know which structure to use.

- **Type 1** verbs: When the first verb is **prospective**, i.e. it looks (or looked) towards the future, the second verb is the consequence or follow-on of the first verb. In this case the second verb can almost always – and with many verbs must – be used in the form of an **infinitive with to**:

- **sample verbs**: *ask, decide, expect, hope, intend, need, plan, promise, want,*

> The secretary **asked to go** home early
> I **decided to take** the train instead of the car.
> I **expect to be** home late tonight.
> I **intend to buy** a new car some time this year.
> We **need to go** to the supermarket before it shuts.
> They **plan to open** three new shops in London this year.
> I **promise not to tell** anyone !
> I **want to learn** English fast !

- **Type 2 verbs.** When the first verb **expresses an emotion, a permanence, or a principle,** the second verb is most likely to be in the form of **a gerund**. Sample verbs: *be afraid / tired of ... etc. , can't stand, detest, dislike, enjoy, hate, keep, keep on, like, love*.

> The secretary was tired **of working** late every evening.
> I can't stand **listening** to that man hour after hour !
> He detests / hates / loves **getting** up early in the morning.
> I very much dislike **having to** tell you everything three times !
> The children really enjoy **going** to see their grandparents.
> Doctor, I keep **getting** this terrible pain in my arm !
> He kept on **reading** until he went to sleep.

Other verbs. Not all consecutive verbs are type 1 or type 2. Several other consecutive or catenative verbs do not fit into either of these types. There are also verbs of **obligation** or **prevention**, and **causative** verbs, which are not really consecutive verbs, as the two verbs are **always separated** in active structures by a noun or pronoun. See ▶ § 1.17.1. Verbs of authority.

Infinitive without to? No Let's not make things complicated! Unlike modals (*will, can* etc.), and with one exception, no consecutive verbs need to be followed by a short infinitive without *to*! The exception is **let**, which **is always** followed by a short infinitive. But apart from a few idiomatic phrases such as ***Don't let go***, or the title of the James Bond novel ***Live and let die***, let is not a consecutive verb, and cannot be directly followed by a second verb. Just a few other verbs **can be** used consecutively and followed by a short infinitive without to (**dare, help, go** ...) but this is optional, an exception to the rule, not another structure.

Take care ! **Non-consecutive verbs.** There are a lot more verbs which, in the **passive**, can be directly followed by a second verb, just like those consecutive verbs that can be used in the passive.

> I **was told to go** home.
> My brother **was taught to speak** English by Mrs. Jones.
> He **was believed to be** in New York at the time.
> The **child was seen getting** into a black car.
> **We were asked** to be ready by six thirty

However **in active statements**, **the direct object** of the first verb, which must be at least a **noun or pronoun,** must come **before** the second verb of which it is also the **subject**.

> The boss **told** me **to go** home.
> Mrs. Jones **taught** my brother **to speak** English.
> People **believed** him **to be** in New York at the time.
> Someone **saw** the child **getting** into a black car.
> They **asked** us **to be** ready by six thirty.

Verbs that are used like this are not consecutive verbs, but normal (non-consecutive) verbs followed by an infinitive phrase or a gerund phrase.

1.11. The verb to be

Forms

Person		Present	Preterite	Present perfect	Past perfect	Future
1st sing.	I	am	was	have been		will be (shall be)
2nd sing	you	are	were	have been		will be
3rd sing	he, she, etc.	is	was	has been	had been	
1st plural.	we	are	were	have been		will be (shall be)
2nd plural	you	are	were	have been		will be
3rd plural	they	are	were	have been		

1.11.1. Functions: to be as a main verb

The verb *to be* is the fundamental verb used to indicate the existence of an entity (person, object, abstraction) or to relate an entity to its qualities or characteristics. In linguistics, it is sometimes known as a *copula*.

Unlike transitive verbs, it does not take a direct object, but a complement, since the subject and complement of the verb *to be* relate to the same entity. The complement of *to be* can be a noun, a noun group, an adjective, or a prepositional phrase.

Examples of usage of the verb to be as main verb

That man **is** the boss.
That man **is** the winner of last year's Nobel Prize for physics.
That man **is** very intelligent
That man **is** in rather a difficult situation
I **have been** here before
She **was** much prettier in her younger days.
The three people **were** all brothers.
The man **had been** in the water for an hour, before anyone found him.
I'**ll be** home by six at the latest, darling !
There'**ll be** at least 200 people at the concert tonight.

1.11.2. Functions: to be as an auxiliary

Progressive or continuous aspect formed with to be

The verb *to be* is used as an auxiliary to denote the **progressive** or **continuous** aspect of an action; it is thus used to form the "present progressive" (§ 1.2.3.) and "past progressive" and other progressive tenses (also called the present continuous and past continuous tenses, etc.). In this case, **be** is followed by the **present participle** of a verb.

We*'re waiting* for the match to begin.
We *have been waiting* for you for two hours.
They *won't be giving* him a prize for his work this time.

Model "stand"	Present progressive	Future progressive	Preterite progressive	Present perfect progressive	Past perfect progressive
1st sing	I am standing	I will be standing	I was standing	I have been standing	I had been standing
2nd sing	you are standing	You will be standing	You were standing	You have been standing	You had been standing
3rd sing	he / she... is standing	He / she ... will be standing	He/ she ... was standing	He / she... have been standing	he / she ... had been standing
1st plural	we are standing	We will be standing	We were standing	We have been standing	We had been standing
2nd plural	you are standing	You will be standing	You were standing	You have been standing	You had been standing
3rd plural	they are standing	They will be standing	They were standing	They have been standing	They had been standing

Other tenses can be formed, including tenses with modal auxiliaries:
examples   *I could have been standing - They must have been standing.*

1.11.3. Passive forms with be

The verb **to be** is also used as an auxiliary to form **passive tenses**. In this case, the auxiliary **be** is followed by the **past participle** of a verb.

Sample verb "Take"	Present simple passive	Future passive	Preterite passive	Present perfect passive	Past perfect passive
1st sing	I am taken	I will be taken	I was taken	I have been taken	I had been taken
3rd sing	It... is taken	He / she ... will be taken	He / she ... was taken	He / she ... has been taken	He / she ... had been taken
Etc					

Other tenses can be formed, including tenses with modal auxiliaries.

Examples

> You could have been seriously injured.
> They must have been told the truth.

1.11.4. Progressive tenses in the passive

As to be is used both to form passive tenses, and tenses with progressive aspect, it follows that it is used *twice* in verb forms that are both passive and progressive.

While a complete range of tenses is theoretically possible, in practice English only has **two passive progressive tenses**, the present progressive passive, and the past progressive passive.

Sample verb "help"	Present progressive passive	Past progressive passive
1st sing	I am being helped	I was being helped
3rd sing	It... is being helped	He / she ... was being helped
Etc.		

1.11.5. Get used instead of be in passive forms

In everyday English, the auxiliary *be* is often replaced by *get* to express a verb in the passive, whether in progressive or simple aspect.

> She *was being / was getting* taken to hospital, when suddenly she felt much worse.
> The computer network is down, as the server *is being / is getting* changed.
> The window *is being / is getting* mended.
> The staff *were being* given their daily instructions.
> Next I *was taken / got taken* to see the director of human resources.

1.11.6. Avoid confusion

Remember that when the auxiliary **to be** is followed by a **present** participle, the verb is in the **active voice**; when it is followed by a **past** participle, the verb in in the **passive voice.**

> The chicken **was eating** its dinner.
> The chicken **was eaten** for dinner.
> They **were telling** the truth, when they said that they knew nothing.
> They **were told** the truth, when the man finally confessed.
> The women **have been asking** to see the managing director.
> The women **have been asked** to see the managing director.

1.11.7. The verb to be as a modal verb

The verb to be is occasionally used as a modal auxiliary; but in this it is a strange verb, as it can have either a value of **futurity**, or a value of **obligation**, or something between the two, **supposition**.

In the first and third persons, it is a modal whose most common value is **futurity**: **in the second person**, its main value is one of **obligation**. However, this distinction is not always true.

Person		Present	Preterite
1st sing.	I	I am to make	was to make
2nd sing	you	You are to make	were to make
3rd sing	he, she, etc.	... is to make	was to make
1st plural.	we	... are to make	were to make
2nd plural	you	... are to make	were to make
3rd plural	they	... are to make	were to make

In other words, while "*I'm* to get a new car next week" would normally mean "*I'm* **going to** get a new car next week" (futurity), "**You're** to go to London next week" would normally mean "You **should** go to London next week" (mild obligation). However, in many cases, ambiguity is possible, even if **context** usually clarifies the meaning.

1. The train **was to** leave at 8 (meaning: The train *was supposed to* leave at 8).
2. I**'m to** work in London next year (I'm *going to / have to* work in London.....).
3. I**'m to** make three of these cakes (I *must / am supposed to* make three.....).
4. He**'s to** stand as candidate for the presidency (He *is going to* stand.....).
5. The children **were to** stay at home that afternoon (The children *were meant* to or *were going to* .....).
6. After that, they **were to** get lost. (After that, they *were going to* get lost).
7. After that, they **were to** go home (After that, *they were supposed to* go home).
8. You**'re to** get better marks next time. (You ***must*** get better marks ....).
9. When you get home, you**'re to** go straight to bed. (When you get home, you *must* go straight to bed).

1.12. The verb to have

Forms functions and usage

The verb **have** is one of the two most frequently used verbs in English. It can be used in three different functions in the sentence.
   1. As a main verb
   2. As an auxiliary verb, and
   3. As a modal auxiliary verb.

1.12.1. Have as a main verb

The verb *to have* is one of the core verbs of the English language, and can be used to express possession ownership or acquisition.

In this usage, it is a transitive verb, and must therefore be followed by a direct object. The direct object of *to have* can be a noun, a noun group, a pronoun or a numeral.

1.12.1.1. *Affirmative forms of the main verb to have*

Person Tense	1st / 2nd sing I / you	3rd sing he, she, etc.	Plural we / you / they
Present.	**have**	**has**	**have**
Future	will have		
Preterite	had		
Present perfect.	**have had**	has had	have had
Past perfect	had had		

1.12.1.2. *Abbreviated forms of have:*

As a main verb, **have** and **has** are **not** normally abbreviated, though shortened forms **'ve** or **'s** are found in some common expressions such as *"I've an idea"*.

Abbreviated forms are more common with the present perfect and past perfect forms, but note that in this case it is the auxiliary that is shortened, not the main verb which always remains **had**. (Example: *We'd all had a good time*). More examples below.

1.12.1.3. *Negative forms of the main verb to have.*

Take care! The normal negative forms of the main verb **have / has** are **do not have** and **does not have**, or their shortened forms. These are <u>not</u> the same as the normal negative forms of the <u>auxiliary</u> or <u>modal</u> verb **have**. The forms *haven't, hasn't, (have not, has not)* etc. are **not** normally used as negative forms of the <u>main verb</u> **have**.

Contracted forms can be used in all styles of English, oral and written, except for the most formal.

Person tense	1st / 2nd sing I / you	3rd sing he, she, etc.	Plural we / you / they
Present.	do not have / don't have	does not have/ doesn't have	don't have
Preterite	did not have / didn't have		
Present perfect.	haven't had	hasn't had	haven't had
Past perfect	hadn't had		

Exceptions: There are some exceptions where the negative form of the main verb *have* uses the negative structure of the auxiliary, notably some common expressions such as *I haven't a clue* (= I don't know) or *I haven't the time*; but even with this second possible exception, it would be more normal to say *I don't have (the) time* or *I haven't got time.*

Examples of use of the verb *have* as main verb

1. I **have** an idea. *(possession)*
2. My father **has** three brothers and two sisters.
3. The doctor **had** a lot of experience.
4. He **has** three Rolls Royces and a Bentley. *(ownership)*
5. Where are the scissors? Do you **have** them?
6. The house **has** eight windows and three doors.
7. **I've had** three phone calls so far today. *(acquisition)*
8. Before getting into his car, he**'d had** six glasses of whisky....
9. "Romeo and Juliet" doesn't **have** a happy ending.
10. I**'ll have** chicken curry with fried rice please.
11. I **don't have** any brothers or sisters.
12. We **haven't had** any complaints so far.
13. If he **hadn't had** those mushrooms, he wouldn't be ill.

1.12.2. Have or have got?

Particularly in spoken English, **have** as a main verb, meaning *own* or *possess or receive* can be consolidated by **adding** the word **got**. This is possible only when **have** means *possess*, in a broad sense of the word, and in the present tense. **Got** however cannot be used in questions or negative statements where the auxiliary **do** is used, nor can it follow a modal verb like **will** or **can**.

Replacing **have** by **get** or **had** by **got** is a different question. Though it is sometimes possible when *have* means *receive* (= acquisition, as in **example 7**), in other cases using **get** or **got** is either **impossible** (as in **examples 8, 10 and 13**), or will change the meaning of what is being said (as in example **3**).

1. I**'ve got** an idea.
2. My father has got three brothers and two sisters
3. *The doctor* **had** *a lot of experience.* (had = possessed)

> The doctor **got** a lot of experience. (**got**= *acquired*)
4. He **has got** three Rolls Royces and a Bentley.
5. Where are the scissors? **Have** you **got** them ?
6. The house **has got** eight windows and three doors.
7. I **got** three phone calls today.
8. Before starting his car, he'**d had** six glasses of whisky.... (*had = drunk*)
9. "Romeo and Juliet" is a tragedy; it **hasn't got** a happy ending.
10. I'**ll have** chicken curry with fried rice please.
11. I **haven't got** any brothers or sisters.
12. We **haven't got** any complaints so far.
13. If he **hadn't had** those mushrooms, he wouldn't be ill. (*had = eaten*)

▶ For more about this, see § 1.14 Get and got

1.12.3. Have as an auxiliary

1.12.3.1. Past verb forms using have

The verb **have** is used as an auxiliary to form the present perfect and past perfect forms of other verbs.

Sample verb "walk"	1st sing	2nd sing	3rd sing	Plural
Present perfect	I have walked	you have walked	he / she... has walked	we / you / they have walked
Past perfect	I had walked	You had walked	He/ she ... had walked	we / you / they had walked
Present perfect progressive	I have been walking	You have been walking	He / she... have been walking	we / you / they have been walking
Past perfect progressive	I had been walking	You had been walking	he / she ... had been walking	We had been walking

Other tenses can be formed, including the **future perfect** (simple and progressive – see §1.4.5.) and tenses with modal auxiliaries. These are not common though they may be useful in some cases.

> I **will have walked** ten miles today by the time I get home. (future perfect simple)
> I **will have been walking** for three hours by the time I get home. (future perfect progressive)
> I **could have been walking** on the beach instead of sitting in the car.
> They **must have walked** all the way home.

1.12.3.2. Negative forms of the auxiliary verb *have*.

The standard negative forms of the <u>auxiliaries</u> **have, has** and **had** are **have not / haven't, has not / hasn't** and **had not / hadn't**.

The contracted forms are normally used in spoken English.

Example: *I haven't finished my lunch*. More examples below.

Take care! Forms using do (***don't have, doesn't have*** etc.) are **never** used as negative forms of the <u>auxiliary</u> verb have, only of the **main** verb have. (see above).

Regional variants:

A speaker from England will tend to say: *I haven't seen it but I hadn't told you,* but a speaker from Scotland might well say: *I've not seen it, but I'd not told you,* or even *I havna seen it, but I hadna told you.*

Ain't

Also note the word **ain't**, a colloquial alternative to both **isn't** and **aren't** as well as **hasn't** or **haven't**, as used in the Rolling Stones' classic hit ***"I ain't got no satisfaction"***.

1.12.3.3. Contracted forms of the auxiliary verb have

As an auxiliary, **have, has** and **had** are frequently contracted to the forms **'ve, 's** and **'d**, when this is possible - i.e. after pronouns - , but it depends on the type of English used.

> - **In written English**, contracted forms are possible but **unusual** after pronoun subjects; contracted forms are **not used** after noun subjects.
> - **In oral / spoken English** contracted forms are **normal** but not essential.
> - After pronoun subjects, even in formal speech, even the Queen of England would be likely to say *"I've had a good day"*, rather than *"I have had a good day."*

However after noun subjects, contracted forms may be heard, even if they would not be written: for example,

A newspaper journalist would write
   "The Prime Minister has appointed a new team."
but a TV journalist would say:
   "The Prime Minister's appointed a new team."

1.12.3.4. Passive forms

Verb forms using the auxiliary **have** can also be put into the passive.

Sample verb "**take**"	**Present perfect passive**	**Past perfect passive**
1st sing	I have been taken	I had been taken
3rd sing	He / she ... has been taken	He / she ... had been taken

Other tenses can be formed, including tenses with modal auxiliaries.

Examples:

> You **could have been** seriously injured.
> They **must have been** dreaming.

Different examples of use of the verb have as an auxiliary

> 1. I **have** finished my lunch / I'**ve** finished my lunch.
> 2. The president **has** chosen his new team.
> 3. The president'**s** chosen his new team *(this form is possible in spoken language, but it would not normally be written)*.
> 4. The children **had** gone home five minutes earlier than usual.
> 5. The captain **had** told his team to play hard in the final minutes of the game.
> 6. The president **has not** yet arrived / The president **hasn't** yet arrived
> 7. Until I lived in London, I **hadn't** been on a double-decker bus.
> 8. **Have** you seen the light Mr. Jones?
> 9. **Hasn't** the rain stopped yet?

1.12.3.5. The verb *have to* as a modal verb

For information on "have to" as a modal verb, see § ▶ 1.15.1. Modals of obligation below.

51

1.13. The verbs to do and to make

Make and Do are among the commonest verbs in the English language. Native English speakers do not mix them up; but they can cause difficulty for speakers of other languages, as many other languages have a single verb that corresponds to *both* do *and* make in English.

Spanish **hacer**, French **faire**, German **machen**, Italian **fare**, Russian **делать**, Portuguese **fazer**.... they can all mean either *do* or *make* in English. And to complicate things even more for non-native speakers, the English language also has the expression *to make do with* !

1.13.1. Meanings and use of do and make

> The fundamental difference between **do** and **make** is that:
> Expressions with **do** generally focus on a **process;**
> Expressions with **make** focus on **the result** of a process.

- **Do** is generally used in expressions that express **actions**:
  Examples: *do the shopping, do your best, do a competition, do something very stupid…*
  In the expression "**do the shopping**", the focus is on the action, i.e. buying things in shops.

- **Make** is generally used in expressions which focus on the **result**, something that is created, acquired or expressed.
  Examples: *make a shopping-list, make a mistake, make lunch, make a lot of noise, make money*
  In the expression *"make a shopping list",* we are not really interested in the process, but in the result, i.e. *the list that exists once it has been written down.*

- **Make** can also imply cause:
  Example: *make something happen.*

Take care! It is not always easy to determine if the meaning of a verb is focused on the action or the result of the action.

1.13.2. Do

The most significant uses of **do** in English are:

- as an **auxiliary** used in negative forms of the simple present tense, as in *I don't speak Latin* (see present tenses).
- Just occasionally **do** is used as an auxiliary in affirmative contexts, notably to add weight to the affirmation, or else to add emphasis to an imperative.

Oh I **don't** like your shirt, but I **do** like your new jacket.
That music's far too loud! **Do** turn the volume down.

- as a **pro-verb**, used to **avoid repeating** a lexical verb, as in:

You know more than I **do**.
I got better marks in the exam than my brother **did**.

- as a **pro-verb** used in questions to **anticipate** the verb that will be used in the answer, as in:

What are you **doing**? / I'm writing a letter.
In this example do anticipates the verb write.

- as a verb denoting action in a limited number of common expressions.

Common English expressions using *do*

To **do** a job / the housework / your homework / the washing up / the shopping etc.
To **do** something wrong / right.
To **do** something very quickly / slowly / clever / stupid / etc.
To **do** your best / To do well
To **do** business with someone

There are also some idiomatic uses of do, including a couple of prepositional uses of the verb to do, notably:

That will **do** meaning *That is enough.*
To **do without**, as in *There was no bread left, so we had to do without it at dinner.*
To **do up**, as in *The house looked very old, but they did it up and now it looks like new.*

1.13.3. Make

The verb *make* usually implies cause or creation. It is used four main ways.

1. As a **causative** verb as in:

> I **made** him tell me all about his holidays.
> The things he said **made** me very angry.

2. As a **standard** verb (a lexical verb) meaning to *create* or *produce* as in:

> Did you **make** that cake yourself?
> I've **made** lunch for everyone.
> They **make** Ford cars in Detroit.
> He doesn't **make** much money working as a barman.

3. In a number of **prepositional** verbs or phrasal verbs (see § 1.18 Prepositional verbs), notably:

> To **make do with** (= to be satisfied by or to manage with)
>   Example: There was no beer, so they *had to make do with* water.
> To **make out** (= to claim, to pretend, or to distinguish)
> To **make up** (= to invent, or to become friends again)
> To **make up for** (= to compensate for)
> To **make it** (= to succeed)
>   Examples: *I made it!!!* or Manchester United *made it* into the semi-finals.

4. As a **verb stressing *result*** or *consequence* or the object (the thing that is made) in a number of common expressions. For example, in the expression *to make a statement*, it is the **statement** we are interested in, not the process of making it.

Common English expressions using **make.**

> To **make** breakfast / a cup of tea / a cup of coffee / a sandwich ... etc.
> To **make** a complaint
> To **make** an exception
> To **make** an excuse
> To **make** a fortune (= to make lots of money)

To **make** friends with
To **make** money
To **make** a mess
To **make** a mistake
To **make** an offer
To **make** peace
To **make** a phone call
To **make** a point
To **make** progress
To **make** a statement
To **make** a success of something
To **make** up one's mind

To **make** out (to distinguish, to see)
To **make** up (to put on makeup, to invent, to become friends again)

1.14. Get *and* got

Forms of the verb get

Person	1st / 2nd sing	3rd sing	Plural
Tense	I / you	he, she, etc.	we / you / they
Present.	**get**	**gets**	**get**
Preterite	**got**		
.Past participle	**got** (or **gotten**, USA only)		

1.14.1. Get as a main verb

The verb *to get* is one of the most common verbs in the English language, and for this reason it has a lot of different meanings.

As a main verb, get plays the part of a "**pro-verb**" in the way that "*it*" is a "**pronoun**". Often it is combined with a particle (preposition or adverb); examples of this are treated below. In such cases, **get** is a full verb in its own right, most commonly with the meanings of *acquire, become, cause or arrive....* but several other meanings are possible (examples 1 - 12 below).

In the **present perfect**, *have got* often functions as a present tense, meaning *have* or *possess* (examples 13 and 14 below).

Get + object + past participle: as in *get it mended* - **get** is used in the meaning of cause (to happen) - (examples 15 - 17 below).

Examples of get as a main verb

1. I'm **getting** a new car tomorrow. (*acquiring, buying*)
2. He **gets** very cross when you ask him personal questions. (*becomes*)
3. I'm **getting** someone to cut the grass. (*finding, employing*)
4. We'll **get** to London at 7.30 pm. (*arrive*)
5. I'm going **to get** top marks in my exam. (*achieve*)
6. I just don't **get** it! (*understand*)
7. If you don't take your pills, you may **get** typhoid. (*catch, acquire*)
8. It's almost six thirty; we really ought **to get going** now. (*start*)
9. I **got** the last two loaves of bread in the shop. (bought, *acquired*)
10. We're **getting** rather cold waiting for you. (*become*)
11. He's just **got** a new job. (*found*)
12. Hello! We're early, but we'**ve got** here faster than expected. (*reached, arrived*)
13. He'**s got** two sisters and a brother. (*has, possesses*)
14. He'**s got** three Cadillacs and a Bentley. (*has, possesses*)
15. I'**m getting** a new suit made specially for my wedding.
16. He **got** his photo taken by a famous photographer.
17. **Have** you **got** everything finished?

Has got or has gotten in American English?

American English **does not** use **gotten** in the **present** meaning of *possess* or *has/have*.

Gotten is the normal **past participle** in American English **only** when the verb get is used in the present perfect, with the meaning of *become* or *reached* or *acquired.*

He's just **got / gotten** a new job. (*found, acquired*)
Hello! We're early, but **we've got / gotten** here faster than expected. (*reached, arrived*)
There's a storm coming; **it's got / gotten** very dark outside. (*become*)
NO! He's **got** / ~~gotten~~ two sisters and a brother. (*has, possesses*)
NO! He's **got** / ~~gotten~~ three Cadillacs and a Bentley. (*has, possesses*)

1.14.2. Phrasal and prepositional verbs with get

Get is the base verb used in a considerable number of phrasal and prepositional verbs in English. Unfortunately there is no way to master and understand them all without learning them either deliberately or through practice.

Here are some of the more common examples:

Two-part verbs: *Get across, get away, get by, get down, get in, get on, get round, get through, get out, get over, get up*

We ought to **get away** by six at the latest. (*depart, leave*)
I'm trying to **get** this **across** simply. (*explain*)
We ought to be able to **get by with** £100. (*manage, succeed*)
Can I **get down**, please.. (*leave the table*)
Get in quickly, it's going to rain very hard. (*go in, enter*)
Peter and Natalia **get on** very well together. (*like each other*)
I can't **get through** this in a week. (*do, finish*)
Get out!. (*Leave, go away!*)
He **got over** COVID-19 quite quickly. (*recovered from*)
I **got round** the problem by using my head. (*avoided, got past*)
I always **get up** late on Sundays. (*get out of bed*)

Three-part verbs: *Get away with, get down to, get on with, get round to*, the meanings should be clear from the examples.

He looks so innocent he could **get away with** murder .
Come on, it's already 8.30, it's time to **get down to** work.
Get on with the job, and stop looking out of the window.
I've got too much work this week, so I don't think I can **get round to** mending your computer too.

1.14.3. Get as passive auxiliary

Get with past participle

Get is often used, particularly in colloquial styles, as a passive auxiliary, in place of **be**. (see § 1.11.) As with other forms of the passive, passive sentences with get are mostly intransitive, though get can also be used in **ditransitive** passives (passives with an object) (Examples 6 - 8 below).

1. Sorry I'm late, the train **got** (was) delayed.
2. My grandfather **got** (was) killed in the war.
3. She's **getting** (being) driven to the ceremony in a big limousine.
4. Survival training includes **getting** (being) dropped in the middle of the desert.
5. We're **getting** (being) picked up at 7.15 tomorrow morning.
6. She **got** (was) given a lovely present by her boyfriend.
7. Everyone **got** (was) clearly told what to do by the team leader.
8. I **got** (was) asked a very difficult question.

1.14.4. Got to - modal auxiliary

▶ For information on "got to" as a modal verb, see the following section Modals of obligation § 1.15.1.1.

1.15 Modal verbs

Modal verbs – definitions

Modal verbs, or modal auxiliaries, are **helper verbs** which affect the meaning of a main verb, by adding a quality to the action, most commonly **possibility, probability, obligation** or **recommendation,** or **futurity** The expression **modal verbs** can be taken in two ways, either as a **syntactical** reference (concerned with their grammatical usage) or else as a **semantic** reference (concerned with what they mean). Syntactically, *have to, need to* and *be able to* are not traditionally classed as modal verbs; however semantically they fulfil the same function, so it is useful and logical to include them in the same chapters.

1.15.1 Modal verbs of obligation

Must, have to, should and *ought to,* and *need to*

There are two types of modal verbs of obligation;

1. those that primarily express a **firm obligation** or **necessity** - **must** and **have to**
2. those that imply **recommendation** or **moral obligation** - **should** and **ought to,** and **need to.**

1.15.1.1 Firm obligation, etc. - must and have to

The verb **must** only exists in the *simple present* and *present perfect* forms.

While the **present** form can express obligation, necessity, certainty or strong probability, the **present perfect** forms *only* express a strongly felt opinion or supposition. See examples in section 1.15.1.2.

All persons	**Present**	Present perfect
Affirmative	must	**must have**
Negative	*must not, mustn't*	**must not have, mustn't have**

If other tenses are required, the speaker or writer must use forms of the synonymous modal verb "**have to**". This modal auxiliary has all normal tenses, including progressive or continuous forms; these are not common, but need to be used in some cases.

Principal tenses	Present	Present perfect	Past	Future
Affirmative	has to, have to	has had to have had to	had to	will have to
Negative *	does not have to, do not have to, doesn't have to don't have to	has not had to have not had to	did not have to didn't have to *	will not have to won't have to
Progressive or continuous	am having to is having to, are having to	has been having to have been having to	was having to were having to	will be having to

* The form "*had not to*" is sometimes used, but it is generally considered to be archaic.

1.15.1.2. *Got to:*

In spoken English, and in the present and preterite forms only, **have to** is often substantiated by the word **got**;
    For example an alternative to *I have to* is *I've got to*.
▶ For more on this, see § 1.14 Get and got.

1.15.1.3. Examples:

Examples of **modals of obligation** being used to express:

    a. Firm <u>obligation</u> or <u>necessity</u>

    b. Certainty or strong probability.

    c. **Must have** only: supposition

---

a1) You **must** see a doctor at once!
a2) I **have to** be at school tomorrow at 8 a.m. I have an exam!
a21) I've **got to** be at school tomorrow at .....
a3) You **mustn't** touch that plate, it's too hot.
a4) I **had to** see a doctor, because I felt very sick.
a5) I **had to** break the window! I lost my key!
a6) The manager isn't here, he**'s had to** go to Paris on urgent business.
a7) Tomorrow the President **will have to** open Parliament.
a8) She**'s having to** move because she can't stand the noise.
a9) I**'m having to** take out this detonator very slowly, to avoid an explosion.
a10) Oh you're so kind! You **didn't have to** do it as well as that!
b1) He **must** be over eighty, he was born in 1938.
b2) If my brother's not in London, he **has to** be in New York.
b3) I've got all the right answers, I **must** be one of the winners!
b4) If I remember correctly, it **has to** be here.
c1) I can't find my laptop, I **must have** left it in the train.
c2) If they're out, they **mustn't have** heard the news.

Take care!

Take care to distinguish correctly between "**had to**" and "**must have**":

*They **had to** go to Washington.*
    = They were obliged to go to Washington.
*They **must have** gone to Washington.*
    = In my opinion, they have certainly gone to Washington.

▶ Other uses of the verb have: see § 1.12 The verb *to have*.
▶ For **word order** with modal verbs in questions, see § 4.2.1.1.

1.15.2. Recommendation or moral obligation -
a) Should and ought to

The verb **should** only exists in the simple present, and present perfect forms.

Forms of should

All persons	**Present**	Present perfect
Affirmative	**should**	**should have** + participle
Negative	should not, shouldn't	Should not have, shouldn't have

The verb **ought to** only exists in simple present and present perfect forms.

Forms of ought to

All persons	**Present**	Present perfect
Affirmative	*ought to*	*ought to have*
Negative	*ought not to, oughtn't to*	*ought not to have, oughtn't to have*

Should and **ought to** are more or less synonymous.

b) Need (to) :

Used affirmatively, **need to** implies strong recommendation; but used negatively it expresses an absence of obligation. There are two negative forms of **need**, either **don't need to** or **needn't**.

Take care! 1. **need** is also used as a main verb followed directly by an object (as in *I need you*). 2. **Needn't** is never followed by *to*.

Examples:

a1) You **should** stop smoking (= You **ought to** stop smoking.)
a2) It's raining hard, the children **ought to** come indoors.
a3) I didn't know you were married! You **ought to have** told me!
a4) If you'd wanted to succeed, you **should have** worked harder at school.
a5) This pullover's got holes in it, I **should** get a new one.
a6) This pullover's got holes in it, I **ought to** get a new one.

> a7) That's awful! You really **oughtn't to have** done that, you know!
> b1) I've been working non-stop for six hours, I **need to** take a rest.
> b2) I think you've got covid….. you **need to** get tested at once.
> b3) Thank goodness, I haven't got covid, so I **don't need to** stay at home
> b4) Thank goodness, I haven't got covid, so I **needn't** stay at home.

Pay attention to the **interrogative** structures used with **ought to, should** and **need**. They are all different!

    Ought I to go to London tomorrow?
    Should I go to London tomorrow?
    Do I need to go to London tomorrow?

1.16. Modal verbs of ability

Modal verbs of ability are used to express two different types of ability:

  Open possibility, generally expressed by forms of **can** or **could**

  Authority or potential ability, usually expressed using **may** or **might**

These verbs are followed by the infinitive without *to*.

1.16.1. Open possibility – can, could and be able to

The verb can only exists in the simple present, simple past (as **could**) and present perfect structures.

All persons	**Present**	Past	Present perfect
Affirmative	can	could	can have + participle
Negative	can not, cannot, can't	could not, couldn't	cannot have

If other tenses are required, the speaker or writer must use forms of "**be able to**". Functioning semantically as a modal verb, **be able to** is an alternative to can when **can** implies ability, though not when it implies permission. It has all necessary tenses, as it is in reality just the verb **to be** followed by the adjective **able**.

The verb **be able to is not used in** progressive or continuous tenses, but the present participle / gerund *being able to* is sometimes used (example a9 below).

Sample tenses	**Present**	Present perfect	Past	Future
Affirmative:	am able to, are able to is able to	has been able to have been able to	was able to were able to	will be able to
Negative; sample forms	am not able to , am unable to	has not been able to has been unable to	was not able to was unable to	will not be able to will be unable to

Can, could and **be able to** are used to express:

- a. Physical or potential <u>ability.</u> (Examples a1 – a8)
- b. **Authority** to do something (by confusion with **may**) – (Examples b1 and b2)
- c. **Can** only: in the present perfect, a past possibility. (Example c1) This is particularly common with negative clauses
- d. **Could:** As well as being used as the past form of *can* **could** can also be used as a modal referring to future time or used in a present perfect structure -- **could have** + past participle, (example d1 - d3).

Examples

a1) I **can** speak three different languages, English, French and Spanish.
a2) He **can't** open the door, it's stuck.
a3) **I'm able to** speak three languages, German, English and Russian.
a4) He**'s unable to** get into his car, he's lost the key.
a5) When I lived in York, I **could** walk to work in five minutes.
a6) If you lose the key, you **won't be able to** get into your apartment.
a7) I **haven't been able to** finish the job, it's too difficult.
a8) In spite long discussions, they **were unable to** reach an agreement.
b1) The policeman says we **can** go in now.
b2) **Can** we please sit down!
c1) They **cannot have** seen the warning sign.....
d1) I **could** see it a minute ago, but I can't see it any longer.
d2) You **could** come and see us tomorrow, couldn't you?
d3) I **could have** finished the whole test if I'd had five more minutes.

Take care!

Be careful to distinguish correctly between "**could not**" and "**cannot have**".

> *They **could not see** the warning sign*
> = They **were unable to see it**, for example, because it was hidden.
> *They **cannot have seen** the warning sign.....*
> = They **must have not seen it**, even though it was there and visible.

1.16.2. Potential possibility or authority
- may and might

The verb **may** only exists in the simple present, past and present perfect forms. The simple past form of **may** is **might**. *Might* is also used in its own right as a present tense modal.

Forms of may

All persons	**Present**	Past	Present perfect
Affirmative	may	might	may have
Negative	may not	might not	may not have

Forms of might

All persons	**Present**	Past	Present perfect
Affirmative	might	might	might have
Negative	might not	might not	*might not have*

Uses of may and might

- a) The modal **may** is used to imply **potentiality** (*limited possibility*) or **authority** to do something. Using the modal **may** is frequently the same as qualifying a statement with the word **perhaps**. Its past form **might** is most commonly found in dependent clauses, notably in reported speech. **Note** that a synonym of **perhaps** is **maybe**.... which is of course composed of the words *may* and *be*. (Examples a1 – a41).

- b) Used in present perfect structures (may + have + past participle), **may** is also used to express **possibility that occurred in a relative past** (something that *perhaps* occurred), i.e. in past time with relation to the present or to some other moment.

- c) **Might** is also used to imply <u>remote possibility</u>, i.e. something that *could just be possible*. In this sense, it is often combined with **be able to**.

- d) Used in present perfect structures (might + have + past participle), **might** is also used to express a <u>hypothetical possibility</u> (affirmative or negative) **in the past**. This is particularly common in type 3 conditional clauses.

- e) **Might** and **may** can both be used to imply politeness or sarcasm.

Examples

a1)	We **may** (perhaps) go to England next year, if we have enough money.
a2)	But of course, we **may** not be able to afford it.
a3)	The policeman said "You **may** go now".
a31)	The policeman told me I **might** go.
a4)	I **may not** be able to get home on time.
a41)	She said she **might not** be able to get home on time.
b1)	I **may have** left my mobile phone on the train.
b2)	It's five o'clock; they **may have** finished by now.
b3)	I **may have** seen something very important.
c1)	I **might** find a job if I'm lucky.
c2)	I think they'll get the contract, but they **might** not.
c3)	I **might** be able to get tickets for the show tonight, it's just possible!
d1)	You're very lucky to be alive; you **might have** died!
d2)	I'm afraid that someone **might have** heard us.
d3)	I **might have** won if I'd run just a little bit faster.
d4)	You **might not have** broken it if you'd been more careful.
e1)	(Please) **may** I say how happy I am to be here!
e2)	**Might** I ask what you are doing?

▶ For **word order** with modal verbs in questions, see § 4.2.1.1.

1.17. Verbs of enabling and obligation

Enablement permission prevention and causation

Verbs of enablement and obligation, or causative verbs, often create problems for students. In English, they have some rather peculiar structures that may not correspond to structures in other languages. Here are the basic rules, to help you master these important verbs.

1.17.1. Verbs of obligation or authority:

allow, ask, authorise, instruct, invite, leave, oblige, permit, require, tell, want etc.

After these verbs, **the second verb is in the infinitive with to.**

> He **told** me **to hurry.**
> They **allowed** us **to leave** the room.
> The man **instructed** me **to come** down.
> The police **required** me **to give** a blood sample.
> I **want** you **to know** I love you.

N.B. With all these verbs, the subordinate clause must be introduced by a **subject**, which is also the object of the main clause: for example, **we cannot say**:

> ~~** The man **permitted to open** the doors **~~
> ~~** I **told not to do** that **~~

All the verbs listed can be easily used in the passive except **want**.

> The singer **was told** to come down.
> He **was invited** to give a concert.
> She **was forbidden** to leave the room.
> I **was required** to fill in a form.
> They **were asked** to sit down.

1.17.2. Verbs of prevention:

1. Stop, prevent, hinder :

These verbs are followed by **"from"** and an **-ing** structure. The word "from" is essential with **hinder**, optional with **stop** and **prevent**.

> He **hindered** us from starting in time.
> He **stopped** me (from) falling in the hole.
> They **prevented** me (from) going out.

Stop is not usually used in the passive, but **hinder** and **prevent** easily accept passive structures:

> The hooligans **were prevented from** making trouble.
> We **were hindered** by the bad weather.

2. Forbid
The verb **forbid** is followed by a **full infinitive** with **to**, just like verbs of obligation above. It can also be used in the passive.

> I'm going to **forbid** the children to stay out after 9 o'clock.
> They **were forbidden** to stay out after nine o'clock at night.

1.17.3. Causative verbs - verbs of direct authority:

1. let, make, have, tell.
Of these verbs, only **let** can be used as a consecutive verb, i.e. followed directly by a second verb. **Make have** and **tell** must always be followed by a noun or pronoun complement; with **make** & **have** the second verb is in the short infinitive **without to**; *tell* is followed by a full infinitive **with to.**

> I told you not to **let go**!
> I **let** him **do** it.
> He **made** me **sit** down.
> **Have** him **tell** you what he saw!

Of these verbs, only one can be used in the passive, **make**.

> I **was made** to take off my skates.

Don't confuse let and **leave**: when followed by an object and a subsidiary clause, **leave** means *abandon, quit*.

> We **left** him **to** get on with his work. (i.e. *we went away*)
>   does not mean the same as
> We **let** him get on with his work (i.e. *we allowed him to....*)

2. Get
With this verb, the second verb form is the full infinitive with *to*.

> I **got** the people **to** read the instructions very carefully.

(▶For more on **got**, see § 1.14.1)

1.18. Phrasal and prepositional verbs
1.18.1. General principles

Phrasal verbs, also called **particle verbs**, are reputed to be the hardest point of English grammar to master. **Why** does one say:

> I **looked it up** on the Internet, *but*   I **looked for** it on the Internet **?**

To answer this question, we need to understand two points

Firstly we have to understand that there are two different verb+particle combinations in English; on the one hand there are **phrasal verbs;** on the other hand **prepositional verbs.** Unfortunately many guides to English use the term "*phrasal verb*" to describe both types, which is not helpful. To avoid this problem, let's distinguish between the two terms.

- A **phrasal verb** (**or particle verb**) is a verb that combines with a **particle.** Particles are prepositions or adverbs, depending on the circumstances, such as *over* in the expression *Why don't you come over tonight !*
- A **prepositional verb** is a verb whose meaning is defined or determined by the **preposition** that follows it, such as *for* in *I looked for it.*

Secondly we need to understand the principle of **separability**.

When a verb is **separable**, verb and particle can be separated by a **direct object**, but not normally by adverbs or adverb phrases (in active sentences).

> **Example:** *I looked it up on the Internet -*

In this case look and up can be separated by an **object**, such as it, but not by anything else such as an adverb.

When a verb is **inseparable**, the **object** cannot come between the verb and the particle or preposition   - though some adverbs may come between them.

> **Example:** *I looked for it on the Internet -*

In this case look and for cannot be separated.... though we could put an adverb between them, such as *desperately*, as in *I looked desperately for it ...*

So which verbs are separable and which ones are inseparable? Fortunately the answers to these questions are not as complicated as is often believed. We can start with three rules.

1. The first rule is that **transitive** phrasal verbs are **separable**.
2. The second is that **transitive** prepositional verbs are **inseparable**
3. The third is that all **intransitive** verbs are inseparable. These rules give us a clear table:

	Transitive (in the active)	**Intransitive**
Phrasal verbs	**Separable** I looked the word *up.* or I looked *up* the word in the dictionary. or I looked it *up* in the dictionary.	**Inseparable** Please *sit down.*
Prepositional verbs	**Inseparable** I **looked** *(in vain)* **for** the word.	

Notes: Separable verbs in active contexts. **Noun** objects **may** come before or after the particle, but **pronoun** objects **must** come between the verb and the particle, as in the example above, *I looked it up*.

In the **passive**, all verbs are inseparable.

The difference between separable and inseparable verbs is not always apparent in active transitive sentences when the object is a **noun**. Indeed if the object is placed after the particle, the difference is not apparent at all, since there is **no difference**. The difference is however perfectly clear when a sentence has a **pronoun** object, or is in the passive, as the following examples show.

With **nouns as objects**	With **pronoun objects**	(Passive - if possible)
The car **ran over** the dog	The **car ran it over**	The dog **was run over** by the car.
The soldiers **ran** over the field	The soldiers **ran** over it.	Improbable.
The editor quickly **looked through** the new book	He quickly looked it through	It **was** quickly **looked through** by the editor.
We **looked** through the window into the garden.	We **looked** through it into the garden.	Impossible
I **got off** all the dirty marks.	I **got them** all **off**	All the dirty marks **were got off** by me. (Improbable)
I **got** off the bus at Bristol.	I **got** off it at Bristol	Impossible

▶ The examples on the **yellow lines** use **phrasal verbs.** The preposition is an **integral part of the verb**, defining its meaning.

▶ The examples on the blue lines either use **prepositional verbs**, where the preposition **determines the meaning** of the verb, but is part of the <u>adverb phrase</u> following the verb; or they are are just a verb followed by a preposition.

Fortunately, verbs like those in the examples above, verbs that can be *either* phrasal or prepositional, are rare. With the vast majority of verbs, there is no choice. The verb is *either* a phrasal verb or a prepositional verb.

1.18.2. Transitive verbs

1.18.2.1 - Transitive phrasal verbs

Almost all transitive phrasal verbs are separable. This means that a **noun object may** come between the verb and the particle, and a **pronoun object must** come between the verb and the particle. There are hundreds of separable phrasal verbs in English. The table below shows the principal root verbs from which separable phrasal verbs can be created, and the principal particles that are used to create them. Almost all combinations of these verbs with the particles indicated will be separable. Note that each root verb will only combine with **certain** particles, **not** all of them.

Principal roots of separable verbs	Sample pronoun object	Main particles used
break, bring, call, check, cut, give, hold, keep, leave, let, look, make, put, run, set, take, think, turn, work, write	it	back, down, in, over, off, on, out, over, round, through, up
Example: Let me check **it** out.		

Examples

With noun objects	With pronoun objects	(Passive if possible)
The referee soon **broke up** the fight. or: The referee soon **broke** the fight **up**.	He soon **broke** it **up**.	The fight was soon **broken up** by the referee.
The robbers **set off** the alarm or: The robbers **set** the alarm **off**.	They **set** it **off**.	The alarm was **set off** by the robbers.

1.18.2.2 - Transitive *prepositional* verbs

All transitive prepositional verbs are **inseparable.** Generally speaking...

1. The preposition defines or limits the meaning of the verb, and is an essential link between the verb and its stated or implied object. Compare: *pay me* or *pay a bill* with **pay for** *lunch.*
2. Often, prepositions serve to form a transitive verb from an intransitive root verb: Examples: *look / look at / look for - wait / wait for - come / come through.*
3. Since transitive **prepositional verbs** are inseparable, the direct object **must** follow the {verb + particle} unit. It makes no difference whether the object is a pronoun or a noun.

Prepositional verbs can be formed from a large number of root verbs, and an almost full range of prepositions.

Sample root verbs	Main prepositions used	Sample object
go, fall, look, think; agree, believe, consist, insist, laugh, pay, result, wait, work.... *etc.*	about, after, at, before, by, down, for, from, in, on, over, of, off, on, out, round, through, to, up, without	**it**
Example: We **went** (**quickly**) **over it** again last night.		

Examples of transitive prepositional verbs in use.

With **noun objects**	With **pronoun objects**	Passive
They **came through** (=*passed*) their exam very well.	They **came through** it very well	*Improbable*
The students **looked intently at** (= *studied*) the text	They **looked intently at** it, or They **looked at** it **intently**.	*Improbable*
Everyone **looked forward to** the event.	Everyone **looked forward to** it.	It was *looked forward to* by everyone.
The prisoners **broke out of** their cells.	They **broke out of** them.	The cells were *broken out of.*

Note that the list of prepositional verbs contains verbs and particles that are *also* used in transitive phrasal verbs, plus some additional prepositions, notably *by,* **for** and *without*.

1.18.3 Intransitive verbs - always inseparable

With **intransitive verbs** there is no distinction between phrasal and prepositional verbs. **All** intransitive verbs with particles (adverbs or prepositions) are **inseparable**. Each of the root verbs below can combine with some of the particles

Principal root verbs	Main particles used
come, fall, go, sit, break, bring, call, check, cut, give, hold, keep, look, make, run, take, think, turn, work	about, by, to, **down, in, over,** **off, on, out, round,** **through, up,** without

It is important to remember that:

- **Intransitive verbs** do not have a direct object, so the {verb+particle} unit of an intransitive verb with a particle will by definition be unbroken.
- In **intransitive verbs**, the particle either narrows the sense of the verb (as in *sit down*), or else creates an idiomatic meaning which is different from that of the root verb (as in *shut up*).
- **Inseparable verbs** cannot be separated by their object, but they can be separated by adverbs.

Here are a few examples of intransitive verbs:

Flight BA04 to New York will **take off** at 12.33.
How did that **come about**?
Covid-19 first **broke out** in China in 2019
Tomorrow morning, we all have to **get up** at 5.30.
Once the King had taken his place, the guests all **sat** *quietly* **down**.

1.18.4. Special cases and exceptions

1.18.4.1 Verbs using *get*

The verb *get* is used in many phrasal and prepositional verbs. Some such as *get off,* are phrasal verbs or prepositional according to their meaning. For more details see §1.14.2 Phrasal and prepositional uses of *get*.

1.8.4.2 Inseparable phrasal-prepositional verbs

As mentioned in section 1.18.2.2 above, **double particle verbs, or phrasal-prepositional verbs, are mostly prepositional** verbs in which the root verb is already a **phrasal verb;** so in reality, the structure of these verbs is **{phrasal-verb} + preposition**. Like simple prepositional verbs, transitive phrasal-prepositional verbs are **inseparable**.

Once this is understood usage should not be hard to follow. Here are some more examples.

Using **nouns**	Using **pronoun objects**	(Passive)
We **made up for** lost time.	We **made up for** it.	Lost time was **made up (for)** (as + *explanation*).
The airline **did away with** tickets	The airline **did away with** them	Tickets were **done away with** by the airline.
The builders **got on with** the work	They **got on with** it.	The work was **got on with** by the builders.

Learning tip: always memorise verbs with a pronoun object, i.e. *look it up*... not just *look up*, *look for it*, not *look for*.

Separable *or* **inseparable: examples to remember.**

Separable:
  I **picked** my friend **up** at the station.
  I **picked up** my friend at the station.
   but **not**: I ~~picked at the station up my friend~~.
Inseparable:
  The fireman **came down** the ladder very carefully.
  The fireman **came** very carefully **down** the ladder.
     but not: The fireman ~~came the ladder down~~ very carefully.

1.19. Irregular verbs.

English has about 150 fairly common irregular verbs. Some of these have the same forms in the preterite and the past participle, for example:

Present	Simple past (preterite)	Past participle
bid	bid (or bade)	bid
let	let	let
put	put	put

Most have forms in which the two past forms are different, for example:

take	took	taken
see	saw	seen
bite	bit	bitten
begin	began	begun

2. The noun phrase
2.1. Nouns : what is a noun?

> A **noun** is a lexical word that represents an **entity** (person, creature, object), a **substance**, a **process** (action, evolution) or an **abstraction** (idea, concept).
> Nouns representing named person/s, entity, or place are called **proper** nouns and are **C**apitalised. Other nouns are known as **common** nouns.

2.1.1. The classification of nouns

Every noun can be classified in three different ways.
Proper or common?   Concrete or abstract?   Count or non-count?

- **Proper nouns:** Nouns representing a named person entity, or place are called **proper** nouns and are **C**apitalised. We also call them "names". **Examples**: *Shakespeare, London, India, Mount Everest, the Titanic, the Olympics, Catholicism, Islam, Google, Gandalf.* They are usually concrete and uncountable. Other nouns are known as or **common** nouns.
- **Common nouns:** Nouns that denote entities or substances (even invisible or intangible substances such as air) are called **concrete nouns**; nouns denoting abstractions or processes are called **abstract nouns**.
- **Common nouns** designating items or abstractions that can be counted are known as **count nouns** (or *countable nouns*), and have both singular and plural forms. Nouns designating generalisations or substances are called **non-count nouns** (or *uncountable nouns*) and are normally only used in the singular.
- Almost all non-count nouns **can** also be <u>used as</u> count nouns in certain circumstances, though most often only in the singular. The distinction between count and non-count nouns is fundamental, as they are not used in the same way.
- ▶ For more on this see count and non-count nouns (§ 2.3.)

Common nouns	Count	Non-count
Concrete	car, cat, ball, man, table, engine, class, road, aeroplane,	water, potassium, cement, air, oil, whisky, concrete
Abstract	idea, noun, attitude, name, song, thought, opinion, victory, quantity, length, kilometre	patience, suspense, life, philosophy, music, , work, economics

Examples of non-count nouns being used as count nouns in defined circumstances:

> **Whisky** is an alcoholic drink. This pub has **fifteen different whiskies**.
> **Work** can be interesting, but **this work** I'm doing is very boring.
> **Love** is all you need; and John had **three loves**, his wife, his kids and his car.
> I love **music**, but I particularly love **the music** of Mozart.

While the plural forms *whiskies*, *works* and *loves* are all possible, such plural forms are uncommon. Generally speaking, non-count abstract nouns, for example *suspense, patience* or *music*, cannot be used in the plural.

2.1.2. Nouns and gender

In English, nouns can either be masculine (referring to men or more generally to male creatures), feminine (referring to women, or more generally to female creatures), or neutral (referring to objects, substances, processes or abstractions.)

Contrary to some other European languages, the *gender* of a noun is **not** reflected in the article or adjective that is linked to it.

Thus one says: a man, a lady, a cat, a decision, this man, this lady

On the other hand, the gender of a noun is reflected in the **third person singular** in **personal pronouns** and in **possessive pronouns and adjectives** relating to it. Thus

> I saw **the boy** > becomes I saw **him**.
> I saw **the girl** > becomes I saw **her**.
> I saw **the film** > becomes I saw **it**.
> This is **Mark's** computer > becomes This is **his** computer
> This is **Mary's** computer > becomes This is **her** computer.
> She was **the film's** director > becomes She was **its** director.

For more details see below: Articles, Pronouns, and Possessives.

2.1.3. The formation of nouns

Many nouns represent primary entities; these are **root nouns** such as:

Apple, Boot, Child, Dog, Egg, Finger, Giraffe, Hand, Island......
There are **no rules** that govern the form of a root noun.
Other nouns, known as **derived nouns**, are formed from verbs, adjectives or from other nouns.

 The formation of derived nouns in English is very easy. This is one of the strengths of the English language! Most frequently, derived nouns are formed from a **root** (not necessarily another existing word, but a "lexeme", a unit of lexical meaning) to which is added a prefix or a suffix. Most endings imply a specific or general meaning.

Here are the most common suffixed used to form nouns in English:
-ion , -ence, -ness, -ment, -ity, -ics, -ing .

Examples

> Action, nation, inflation, discussion - with *-ion*
>
> Patience, maintenance, conscience - with *(i)ence* or *-(i)ance*
>
> Madness, emptiness, loneliness, greatness - with *-ness*
>
> Parliament, instrument, apartment, containment, - with *-ment*
>
> Community, commodity, validity, - with *-ity*
>
> Physics, economics, analytics, statistics, logistics - with *-ics*
>
> Farming, marketing, beginning, ending, with *-ing*

2.1.4. Nouns in the plural

Pluralizing nouns in English is very simple. With just a few exceptions, the plural of all English nouns is formed by adding the letter "**s**".

Exceptions to the general principle:

Nouns in s, sh, ss, ch or z,

When the singular of an English noun ends in **s, sh, ss, ch** or **z**, the plural is normally formed by adding **–es.**

Examples: Bus > buses (not ~~busses~~ !), Bush > bushes, Match > matches, Mass > masses, Buzz > buzzes,

With some words ending in **s**, the plural and singular are identical.
Examples: A series > two series, a means > two means > a species > two species.

Nouns ending in -f.

With **some** (but not all) nouns ending in a single **-f**, the plural is formed by replacing the final **-f** by **-ves**.

Examples: Half >halves, hoof > hooves, thief > thieves but Roof > roofs, belief > beliefs
The same goes for words ending in **-fe** (or -ef).
Examples: Knife >knives, life > lives, thief > thieves.

Words ending in -is

With words like analysis, hypothesis, the plural is formed by replacing the final **-is** by **-es**, **Examples**: analysis > analyses, hypothesis > hypotheses, crisis > crises etc. Note how the plurals are pronounced:
  Singular: ['krai sis], plural: ['krai si:z]

Some words derived directly or supposedly from Latin or Greek

In some cases, the original Latin or Greek ending is used.
Cactus > cacti, Medium > media, nucleus > nuclei, criterion > criteria, stimulus > stimuli etc.

A few irregular nouns

A very small number of common English nouns have irregular plurals. Man > men , woman > women , child> children, mouse > mice, foot> feet, tooth > teeth ...

Animals and fish

For some animals, some birds, and a lot of fish (including the word **fish**), the plural is - or may be - **the same** as the singular.

A bison > two bison, a deer > two deer(s), a fish > two fish, a perch > two perch, a salmon > two salmon, a sheep > two sheep, a grouse > two grouse etc.

Most other animals and birds have regular plurals: two horses, two cats, two dogs, two pigs, two pigeons, two eagles etc.

Nouns of nationality in the plural

Nouns of nationality ending in **–sh -ch -ese** or **-ss** do not take any plural ending; they are **invariable**. Other nouns of nationality obey the general rules for plurals.

Examples: The English, the Scottish, the Spanish, the French, the Dutch, the Swiss, the Portuguese, the Chinese, the Japanese, the Lebanese....

But: The Americans, the Australians, the Finns, the Swedes, the Russians, the Poles, the Brazilians, the Serbs, the Greeks, the Moroccans, the Afghans, the Pakistanis, the Ukrainians, etc.

2.1.5. Collective nouns - singular or plural?

Collective nouns, or **group** nouns, are nouns such as **family, government, class** or **committee**, which refer to groups of people or things.

While these are technically singular nouns, they are commonly used as if they were plurals, specially in British English.

Examples: in this example, both alternatives are acceptable:

> The Government **have** decided to increase security measures.
> The Administration **has** decided to increase security measures.

In the next example, the first option is grammatically acceptable, but improbable.

> The whole class **is** going to take the test again *sounds a bit strange; prefer*
> The whole class **are** going to take the test again.

because in this case, it is clear that each student of the class will be taking the test again *individually*. At least, that is what the teachers intend should happen!

Sometimes a plural is essential, even in American English, for example:

> My family **are** immigrants.

We could not possibly say

> ~~My family is immigrants~~ or (even worse!) ~~My family is an immigrant~~.

In this case, it is **context** that requires a plural verb. In other cases, a singular verb will be possible:

> My whole family is / are coming to see me this weekend.

2.1.5.1. What is the rule?

Essentially, notably in British English, if the **collective unit** - *family, government, committee, club, class* or whatever is being treated as a **single** entity, doing things **collectively**, then we will usually put the verb into the **singular**.

If, on the other hand, the collective unit is being seen as a **group** of **individuals**, each doing things as an **individual**, then we tend to use a **plural**. So ...

> The committee **has** decided .... gives the impression that the committee has made a **unanimous** decision.
> The committee **have** decided .... gives the impression that the members of the committee have all (or mostly) decided of their own **individual** free will.

In modern **American** usage, people tend more often to use a singular verb with collective nouns, though even in the USA this is not always the case.

A special case

> The word **police** is **always** used in the plural. We cannot say: ~~the police is~~....

2.1.5.2. Collective proper nouns (names)

Corporate names, like **Google** or **Facebook** or **Apple**, are a specific type of collective noun. They are used in the same way as the common nouns shown in the examples above, sometimes as singulars, sometimes as plurals.

> We found out today that Google **are** backing up their Location API
>   *(Washington Post, May 2008)*
> So Google **is** good and bad in one sentence for Donald Trump
>   *(Washington Post, Sept 2016)*

And here are two sentences from the same writer in the same article published in the *Guardian* newspaper in Nov. 2011

> Microsoft **is** investing massively .... but Microsoft **are** still selling copies of Word.

Take care! *Agreement*

When a collective noun is used as a **plural**, the pronouns used to refer back to is must be *they / them / their.* When a collective noun is used as a **singular**, the pronouns used to refer back to is must be *it / its.*

Examples

> In **its** monthly report, the committee **says** that the situation is getting better.
> In **their** monthly report, the committee **say** that the situation is getting better.

2.1.5.3. List of important collective nouns

There are at least 100 nouns that can be used as collective nouns, but only a small number of them are commonly used, and need to be remembered; here are twenty of the most important:

> army   audience   class   club   committee   company   congregation
> corporation   council   family   firm   group   jury   majority   minority
> parliament   public   police   school   team

2.2. Types of noun phrase

A **noun phrase** or **noun group** is a group of words describing or qualifying the noun or pronoun that is the key element in the group. Noun groups can vary in size from a single letter, the pronoun *I*, to a long complex rambling phrase with dependent clauses.

Here are the six essential structures, with examples.

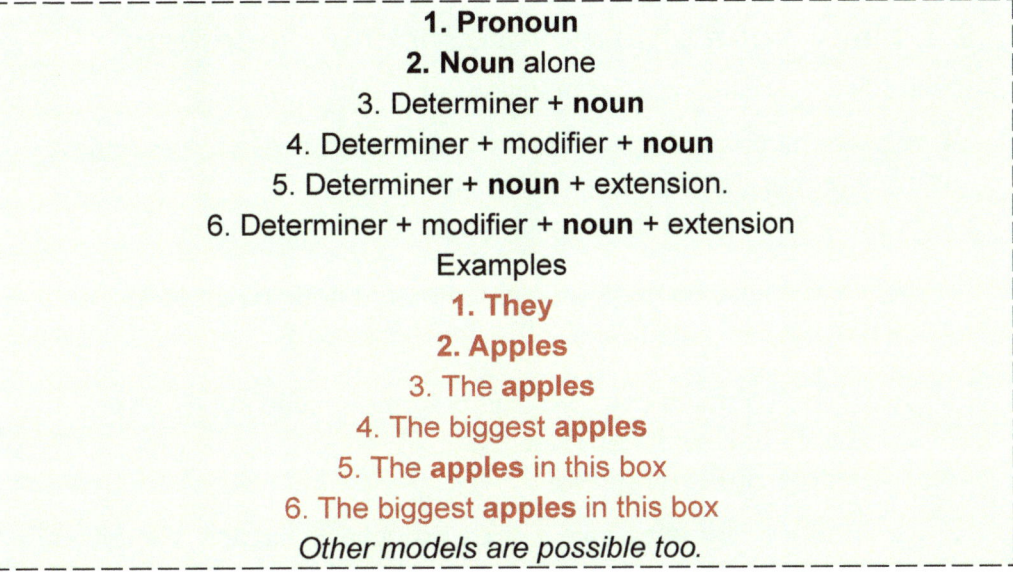

Two simple "rules" govern the use of the noun phrase in English.

2.2.1. Most noun phrases consist of at least two elements

Unless a noun is used in a generalising sense (see articles), or is just a pronoun, a noun phrase consists of at least the following elements: a **determiner** and a **noun**.

A **determiner** is one of the following: an **article** (*the, a, an, some, any*),
- a **quantifier** (*no, few, a few, many,* etc.),
- a **possessive** (*my, your, whose, the man's,* etc.),
- a **demonstrative** (*this, that, these, those*),
- a **numeral** (*one, two, three* etc.)
- or a **question word** (*which, whose, how many,* etc.).

Except in some very rare cases, a noun can only be preceded by **ONE** determiner:

Examples: the man, some women, a few dogs, your horse, the man's horse* , that car, whose money, how many bottles?

* In the example, **the man's horse*** there appear to be two determiners before **horse**, but in fact there is only one: the determiner before **horse** is "**the man**", in which the article *the* is the determiner of the word **man**.

2.2.2. Many noun phrases also include "modifiers"
There are five essential types of modifier:

A **modifier** can be an **adjective**, an **adjectival phrase**, a **secondary noun**, a prepositional phrase or a relative clause.
The principal noun in a noun group is called the **head noun**.

1. **Adjectives** are normally placed before the head noun: as in **the Great Gatsby** (▶ See § 2.9. Adjective order)

2. **Adjective phrases** usually come before the head noun: as in:
    a **black-and-white striped** vest
    a **rather tight-fitting** dress

3. **Secondary nouns** behave exactly like adjectives, and come before the head noun:
    a **beer** glass, the **police** inspector, a **London** bus

4. **Prepositional phrases** and ...

5. ... **relative clauses** follow the head noun, as in:
    the students **in our class** or the girl **who gave me her phone-number**.

Put all this together, and we get a **complex noun group**, such as:

> *The* **nice old-fashioned police inspector with white hair, who was drinking his beer,** *was Mr. Morse.*

2.2.3. Some common exceptions
Sometimes an adjective or an adjectival phrase will follow the noun, or appear to do so. There are three cases that need to be noted:

A very few adjectives always follow the noun: **concerned** (in the sense of "being talked about"), and **involved** (in the sense of "participating", or "being present") are the two common ones.

Other participial adjectives (such as **left, remaining, missing**) appear to be used as adjectives that follow the noun; in reality, they are elliptical forms of a relative clause that has become reduced to a single word.

Adjectives follow the noun when the adjectives themselves are post-modified (defined) by a following phrase.

Examples.
There's been an outbreak of flu, but there are only fifteen people concerned.
After the fight, the police arrested the men involved.
Oh look! there is only one chocolate left!!
We can't go yet!! There are still three people missing.
There was a crowd bigger than last year.
  Note that in this case, we could also say:
There was a bigger crowd than last year.
  But not
There was a ~~bigger than last year~~ crowd.

For more examples see § 2.9.3.1 Attributive adjectives

2.3. Count nouns and non-count nouns

In English, as in many other languages, nouns are divided into two categories, known as **"count nouns"** and **"non-count nouns"**. It is important to distinguish between these two groups.

2.3.1. Count nouns

Sometimes called "countable nouns", these are nouns that refer to things that can be multiplied or counted, for example:

- one man, two trees, three things, four faces, five films, six shops, seven sisters, and so on.

2.3.2. Non-count nouns

These are nouns that refer to generalisations, abstractions, concepts or substances, things that cannot be put in the plural; for example.

- water, oxygen, eternity, psychology, anger, politics, heat, alcohol.... and so on.

So far, so good! That is relatively simple to follow. **Concrete** objects and items can be counted, **concepts** and **abstractions** cannot. Unfortunately, this easy distinction does not take into account all nouns.

The Problem:

The problem is that there are a lot of nouns that are *either* **count nouns** *or* **non-count nouns** , depending on the circumstances.

2.3.3. Usage

Count nouns and **non-count** nouns are not used in the same way. Most importantly there are the questions of **determiners** or articles (*the, a an, some* and *any,* etc.) and **quantifiers**. The essential rules are not complicated:

> **RULE 1 ▶**
> **Count nouns must** have a determiner of some kind in the singular. **In the plural,** count nouns require a determiner if they are used with a restricted value, no determiner if they are used as generalisations.

Examples in the singular
You can say a table, this table, my table, one table, etc. but never just "table".

Examples in the plural
You say "tables" (or "all tables") if you mean *all tables in general,* but "the tables" or "these tables", etc., if you are referring to just *certain tables,* but not *all tables*.

Examples in context:

> Usually, tables have flat surfaces, but **the** tables in this café don't.
> Buses are big vehicles, but **the** buses in London are enormous.

> **RULE 2 ▶**
> **Non-count** nouns do not have a determiner in the singular. They are **not used in the plural**

Example: Oxygen is essential for life.

In cases where non-count nouns are used with a determiner, this is because they are being used with a restricted or count value.
For example: **This** oxygen is contaminated.

2.3.4. Problem: nouns that are either count nouns or non count nouns

There are a lot of nouns that are *either* **count nouns** *or* **non-count nouns**, depending on the circumstances.

In their **non-count** form or value, they are generalisations, in their **count noun** form or value their meaning is restricted or slightly different. Look at these examples:

> We all like **beer**, so let's order **three beers**.
> **Air** is vital for life, but **the air** in this room is very unpleasant.
> Radiators should produce **heat**, but **the heat** from that radiator is minimal!
> **Philosophy** is complicated, specially when there are **several different philosophies** about the same situation.

In the examples above, the first time the noun is used with a **non-count** generalising value, beer, air, heat, philosophy.

However the second time these nouns are used they have the restricted value of **count nouns**: for this reason, they must be introduced by a determiner; in the examples, the determiners are a numeral (*three*), two articles (*the*) and two demonstrative determiners (*this* and *that*).

> three beers, the air in this room, the heat from that radiator, several different philosophies.

The fact that some nouns can have either a non-count value or a count value does not always mean that we can actually count them! **Many abstractions** cannot be put in the plural; for example

> We **could never** say ~~There are two different airs in these two rooms~~.
> we **cannot** say ~~musics~~ or ~~patiences~~
> though as the examples show, we can say *several different philosophies*.

It is **context** that will usually indicate whether a noun is being used as a **count noun** or a **non-count** noun.

2.3.5. Quantifiers with count and non-count nouns

The choice of certain quantifiers (▶ see § 2.6) such as *much / many, few / little, some* and *any* depends on whether a noun is a **count noun** or a **non-count** noun.

With **count nouns** in the **plural**, the quantifiers to use are *many, few / a few,* and *some**. Obviously, quantifiers cannot be used with **count nouns** in the singular.

> **Many people** speak English.
> **Few animals** escaped from the forest fire.
> **A few animals** escaped from the forest fire. (*This does not mean the same!*)
> The old man was found by **some children**.

*Some is replaced by *any* in negative and interrogative contexts.

With **non-count** nouns in the singular, the quantifiers to use are *much, little / a little,* and *any.* And remember, **non-count** nouns cannot be used in the plural!

> There wasn't **much water** left.
> There was **little food** left in the house. (*Meaning* not much food)
> There was **a little food** left in the house. (*Meaning* a small amount of food)
> There wasn't **any food** left in the house.

2.4. Pronouns

Definition of a pronoun:
A **pronoun** is a little word that stands **in place of** a noun, a phrase or even a clause, in order to avoid repetition. It agrees in number and gender with the noun, phrase or clause that it replaces, which is called the *antecedent*. The pronoun refers to its logical antecedent in a sentence or paragraph, or in the context of dialogue. Within a sentence, the logical antecedent is most often the preceding or most recent noun. Occasionally the "antecedent" can come after the pronoun referring to it.

2.4.1. Personal pronouns

Personal pronouns in English are fairly easy to master. However it is important to remember that for the third person singular, the choice of pronoun depends on the **gender of the antecedent**: *he* (etc.) if it refers to a man or male or unknown person, *she* if it refers to a female, and *it* for everything else.

The feminine pronouns *she / her / hers* are only used with **humans** (*a lady,* etc.), or with a few animated or moving creatures or objects to which the English language can give a quality of femininity (examples *dog, cat, boat*). The object pronoun is also used after prepositions.

♣ Do not confuse **possessive pronouns** (used **in place of** a noun) **with possessive adjectives** - in the final column - (which **precede** a noun).

	Subject pronoun	Object pronoun	Possessive pronoun	Possessive adjective
1st person sg.	I	me	mine	my
2nd person sg.	you	you	yours	your
3rd person sg.	he, she, it, one	him, her, it, one*	his, hers, its, –	his, her, its, one's
1st person pl.	we	us	ours	our
2nd person pl.	you	you	yours	your
3rd person pl.	they	them	theirs	their

Examples: Pronouns are in bold, their antecedents are underlined. Possessive adjectives are in blue.

> Look at that <u>man</u>. Can you see **him**? **He**'s over there, and that's **his** wife with **him**.
> There are two bikes in <u>Peter's</u> garage; the green bike is **his** and the blue one is **mine**.
> We've lost **our** way; can you help **us** please?
> Have **you** seen **my** <u>phone</u>? I can't see **mine**, but **yours** is over there.
> **One** should always bring a map with **one**, in case **one** loses **one's** way.
> <u>I</u> like **our** new <u>house</u> but I don't like **theirs**; and I didn't like **their** old one either

2.4.1.1. The specific case of *one*

The word **one** causes problems not just for students, but for linguists too. Unlike other pronouns, **one** can be used *like a noun*, to replace a previously mentioned noun. In the last example given above, we find the phrase,

> ... and I didn't like **their old one** either

one is not being used as a pronoun, since it is preceded by a determiner (*their*) and an adjective (*old*). It is not a noun either, as it has no intrinsic meaning outside of its context. Swan, in *Practical English Usage* defines **one** as a "substitute word"; others call it a "pro-form". But whatever term we use to describe it, **one** is a special case.

In examples of this type, **one** behaves exactly like a noun, and can be assimilated to a count noun with regard to its usage in the sentence.

2.4.1.2 Reflexive and emphatic pronouns

English has a set of **reflexive pronouns** on the model *myself, yourself, himself,* etc. These are required when a **direct, indirect, or prepositional pronoun complement** of a verb refers back to the subject, as in:

> He convinced **himself** that the exam would be too difficult.
> Since I work for **myself**, I can give **myself** a pay rise.
> We're going to treat **ourselves** to a special holiday after Covid.
> Have you hurt **yourself** badly ?

Reflexive pronouns can also be used as **emphatic** pronouns, longer forms of personal pronouns that can be used for emphasis either **in place of**, or else **in addition to,** a personal pronoun or noun.

> **I myself** do not actually agree with his version of the story.
> Do it **yourself**
> I could not find **the book itself,** so I bought a similar title.

Occasionally an emphatic pronoun is used to emphasize a pronoun that is linked with a noun.

> Peter **and myself** work together as a team.
> Do you mean that it was given **to your father and yourself**?

But this is not always considered as good style; a normal pronoun, as in *Peter and I,* will often be considered more acceptable.

Note that while English has **reflexive pronouns**, it does not use reflexive **verbs**. For example there is no English reflexive equivalent of Spanish *lavarse* or French *se laver,* (= *wash*, not *wash oneself),* nor of German *sich freuen* (= *be happy*) except when used for special emphasis.

2.4.1.3. Indefinite pronouns

There are other pronouns similar to personal pronouns, and generally used like personal pronouns; these are indefinite pronouns or impersonal pronouns: they include words such as *someone, anyone, anything, whoever,* (see also § 2.6.1.3.), and even **numbers** or **quantifiers used as pronouns**, such as *many, enough* or *plenty* or *all.*

Examples

> **Someone** told me you're going to New York next week.
> I can't see **anything.**
> **Whoever** said that was obviously not telling the truth.
> I ordered six boxes, but I've only received **three.**
> **Plenty** was said at the meeting, but the directors couldn't agree.
> He can say complete nonsense, but **many** will still believe him.
> His ideas are complete nonsense, and **few** believe him.
> **Enough** is **enough.**
> **All** is not lost…… **All** you need is Love.

2.4.1.4. Gender neutral pronouns

Sometimes we need to use a third-person singular pronoun to refer to a person, without knowing if the person is male or female, or without wanting to specify the gender. For obvious reasons, we can't use **he** or **she**; but we can't use **it** either, as it is not a gender-neutral personal pronoun, but refers to an object. The classic solution in English is to use **they / them / their** as a singular pronoun: note however that while these pronouns can take on a singular meaning, they are still used in the normal way, as if they referred to a plural entity.

Avoid using the sometimes-used "his or her": this is not considered to be good style, even if it is just occasionally necessary.

Examples

> If someone rings, tell them to call back later.
> If anyone tries to open the safe, they'll get a big surprise.
> Each member of the committee gave their opinion.
> I saw a person leave the building, but I don't know if they were male or female.

2.4.1.5. The expletive pronoun there

There is known as an **expletive pronoun** or *dummy* pronoun; this means that it does not refer to a noun or antecedent that has already been mentioned; it refers to a noun object or complement that **has not yet been specified**. It is a third person pronoun, but can be either used as a singular or as a plural, depending on the noun to which it refers. There is normally only used with the verb **be**, it can be used with any tense of the verb **be**, including **be** preceded by a modal verb. Just occasionally it can be used with certain other verbs, such as **go, live, stand** or **appear**.

Examples

> There was an enormous explosion.
> There are thirteen mistakes in your spelling test.
> I think that there is a hole in my bucket.
> I think that there are some people coming.
> There was a strong smell of smoke in the room.
> There will be no prizes for students who fail the exam.
> There can be no doubt that many top footballers get paid too much.
> There must be a faster way than that.
> Is there any point in filling in all these long forms?
> In the town where I was born (there) lived a man….
> Look! There goes Peter.
> There appear to be three different types of fish in this pond.
> Beside the cottage there stood a very old oak tree.

2.4.1.6. Interrogative pronouns.

See [§ 4.2.1.](#) **Word order in questions**.

2.4.2. Relative pronouns & adjectives

Who, which, that, whoever, what *and others*

See also § 4.6. **Relative clauses** and § 4.2.1. **Interrogative pronouns and determiners.**

2.4.2.1. Relative pronouns - Functions and forms

In their most common usage, relative pronouns introduce a relative clause - either as a subject *(who, which, that)* , or as a direct object (*whom, which, that*), or in the context of a prepositional phrase *(to whom, with which, by which,* etc.). They are called "**relative**" because in a declarative sentence, they **relate** to a noun that has normally just been mentioned.

The most common and most recognised relative pronouns are **who, whom, whose, which** and **that**.

Relating to ▶	Animate (person).	Inanimate (thing).	Either
Subject pronouns	who	which	that
Object pronouns	Whom (who[1])	which	that (or omission)
Pronouns after prepositions	(to, with, by...) whom	(to, with, by...) which	
Possessive relative pronouns	*These do not exist*		
Possessive relative adjectives	whose	of which	whose

Note 1. The case of whom: in many varieties of spoken English the **object pronoun** whom is disappearing, replaced by **that**, or omitted. The word whom survives nonetheless in standard written English, and after prepositions.

Whom has disappeared most notably from direct questions. Few native English speakers would ask *Whom did you see yesterday?* Most would ask: *Who did you see yesterday?*

Examples

This is the man *who* sold me a stolen mobile phone.
There were several people at the party, *whom* I'd never met before.
There were a lot of people (*that*) I'd never met before
The machine, *which* had been running non-stop for 3 days, just stopped.
The machine, *that* had been running for 3 days, just stopped.
I know the man *to whom* you were talking.
I was in a complex situation, *from which* I could see no way out.
The events *that* occurred on Friday were rather alarming.

Take care! The word **whose** is never found on its own at the start of a relative clause: however it can be used as a **possessive relative adjective**, qualifying a noun.

Examples

The President, *whose* wife was a film star, was not very popular.
He found a very old statue *whose* age was impossible to determine.
We cannot say
~~This is my elder brother, whose I was talking.~~
We have to use the prepositional form with *of* (or another preposition):
This is my elder brother *of whom* I was talking.

2.4.2.2. Relative uses of what, whatever *etc.*

1. What as a nominal relative pronoun

What is used as a "**nominal relative pronoun**" (also called "free relative pronoun"). It is a single word which combines the antecedent (stated or implied) and the relative pronoun. Thus it corresponds for instance, to French *ce que* or Spanish *lo que, el que* etc.

Examples

After *what* happened yesterday, you ought to be more careful.
You'll have to manage with *what* you can find.
What he said was rather interesting

2. Whoever, whatever, whichever as nominal relative pronouns

Though less common than *what*, **whoever whatever** and **whichever** are all used as nominal personal pronouns, standing in the place of a noun + relative clause.

Examples

Whoever heard such an ridiculous argument ?
    Meaning: Is there any person who heard such a ridiculous argument ?
Whoever lost the key ought to find it again pretty quickly.
    Meaning: The person who lost the key ought.....
Whatever you say, I'm not going to change my opinion.
    Meaning: You can say anything that you want, but I'm....
We'll give the prize to **whoever** gets the right answer first.
You'll have to manage with **whatever** you can find.
He'll take **whichever** he prefers.

3. Whichever and whatever as relative adjectives

Whichever and **whatever** - but **NOT** *whoever* - can also be used as relative adjectives, standing before a noun.

Examples

Whichever team wins, he'll be a happy man.!
    Meaning: The team **that** wins can be one or the other, and he'll.
We'll have to stay in **whatever** hotel we can find.
    Meaning: We'll have to stay in any hotel **which** we can find
My Dad's promised to buy me **whatever** laptop I want if I pass my exam.

2.4.2.3. *Whose, what* & *which* in questions

Whose, what and **which** can be used as relative **adjectives** (preceding a noun) or relative **pronouns** (in place of a noun), at the start of a direct or indirect question. (see § 4.2.)

Examples.

Whose is this bag?
Whose bag is this?
I know *whose* bag this is.
I know *whose* this is.
I asked him *what* languages he spoke.
I asked him *what* he was doing.
I don't know *which* train to take.
The President knows *which* people he wants to talk to.
Nobody could understand to *which* laws he was referring.

2.4.2.4. *When, why, where* and *how*

Many students are surprised to learn that **when, why, where** and **how**, and also the longer forms **whenever, wherever** and **however**, also function as nominal relative pronouns. As relative pronouns, they are used to replace a longer phrase that would include a standard relative pronoun such as **whom** or **which**.

Examples

> We don't know **when** he's coming.
> *Meaning:* We don't know the time **at which** he's coming.
> Can you explain **why** you did that?
> *Meaning:* Can you explain **for what** reason you did that?
> I can't remember **where** I left my car.
> *Meaning:* I can't remember the place **in which** I left my car.
> In the town **where** I was born, lived a man[1] who sailed to sea.
> *From the Beatles' song Yellow Submarine.*
> I hope you know **how** to mend it!
> *Meaning:* I hope you know the way **in which** to mend it?
> **Whenever** his son comes to stay, they go out to a good restaurant.
> *Meaning:* **Each time that** his son comes....
> **Wherever** he goes, he leaves a trail of damage behind him.
> *Meaning:* In **every place to which** he goes, he leaves .....
> **However** I try, I can't get the right answer.
> *Meaning:* In spite of all the ways in **which** I have tried, I can't get...

2.4.3. Relative adverb: **however**

However can also be used as a relative adverb, qualifying an adjective or adverb.

> **However** hard I try, I can't manage to find the right answer!
> *Meaning:* I can't find the answer even if I try in ways which are very hard.
> We'll have plenty of food **however** many people actually come.
> *Meaning:* The number of people who come is not important, we'll have...

---

1. *Lived a man...* Why is the subject after the verb? Because this is poetry, where word order is not always respected. Also, because *lived* means *there lived,* so the real subject is not *a man*, but the expletive pronoun *there* (see § 2.4.1.5 above)

2.4.4. Demonstrative pronouns and adjectives

2.4.4.1. Demonstrative pronouns

1. There are four demonstrative pronouns in English, two in the singular, and two in the plural; they indicate either proximity (*this, these*), or distance (*that, those*).

	Proximity	Distance
Singular	This	That
Plural	These	Those

It is important to understand what is meant by **proximity and distance**. The notion of proximity can be **grammatical** (referring to something close in the sentence), **spatial** (something close to the speaker) or **temporal** (close in time).

Examples

This is her car, and *that* (further away) is mine.
I don't like *these* (in front of me) but I do like *those* (further away).
Our car has broken down, and it's snowing. *This* (the situation in which we find ourselves) is not a good situation.
He wrote about many places, including some small Greek islands; *these* (direct antecedent in the sentence), he said, were his favourite places.
That (= what you have just said) is not a very intelligent idea.

2. Demonstrative pronouns <u>cannot</u> be preceded by adjectives nor by possessives, but **that** and **those** can be followed by prepositional phrases starting with **of** or **in** or other prepositions. See possessive structures below.

We cannot say *Peter's those,* nor *His that* nor *blue these*; we have to say *Those of Peter*, or *that one of his*, or *these blue ones*.

2.4.4.2. Possessive structures: the demonstrative pronoun followed by "of"

> ▶ First note this important rule:
> **This** and **these** are never followed by **of**:
> For example, we can **not** say:
> ~~My apple is ripe, this of my sister is not.~~

In possessive structures, usage depends whether we are dealing with attribution or possession.

With attribution

The only normal structure with demonstrative pronouns is to use **that of** or **those of**:

> His reputation was bigger than **that of** Elvis.
> While Japan's development was rapid, **that of** Singapore was even faster.
> The title of his first book was "Blue Waves", **that of** the second was "Deep Oceans".

With possession

The most common structure, particularly in spoken English, is to use .....'s or (...'s one(s)).

> My books are new, John's (ones) are old.
>   **Not**: ~~My books are new, those of John are old~~
> Our shirts are white: the other team's ones are red.

That of / those of tend to be only used in **formal** contexts (▶ see § 4.8. Style) , particularly written English:

> The first tourist's papers were in order, but **those of** the remaining tourists were not.

2.4.4.3. Demonstrative pronoun phrases

Demonstrative pronouns (most commonly **those**) can be the headwords of phrases in which they are followed by various prepositions or by a relative clause.

In Demonstrative pronoun phrases, the singular demonstrative pronouns **that** and **this** must normally be reinforced by the addition of **one** to become **this one** or **that one**. This is also possible for **these ones** or **those ones** (but the *one* is not essential).

> Look at those paintings: I prefer **those / those** (ones) on the left.
> This book is mine, but **that one on the table** is yours.
> *We cannot say:* ~~This book is mine, but that on the table is yours.~~
> All **those in** favour, raise your hand.
> I like **these** (ones) **with the strong peppermint flavour**.
> Take as many as you want; **those that are still here tonight** will be destroyed.
> **Those who have finished their project** can go home.
> All **those who want to help** should be here tomorrow morning at nine.
> Look at **these (ones) that I made yesterday**.

2.4.4.4. Demonstrative adjectives

▶ **This (these)** and **that (those)** can also be used as demonstrative adjectives: the same principles of proximity and distance apply.

Examples

> **This** book is mine, **that** book is yours.
> **These** students come from Paraguay.
> I really like **those** new trains they're using now.

"**One**" is sometimes used as a pro-form, to avoid repeating a noun.

> **This** book is mine, **that one** is yours

or even (if the context makes it quite clear what is being referred to)

> **This one** is mine, **that one** is yours.

The definite article **the**, rather than a demonstrative adjective, can also be used with a demonstrative value

> **This one** is mine, yours is **the one** on the table.

2.5. Articles

Articles belong to the larger category of words known as **determiners**. Unlike other common types of determiner (*numbers, demonstratives, quantifiers*), articles cannot stand alone. They must be followed by a noun.

2.5.1. Article usage

> **The basic rules:**
> Basically, the rules for using articles in English are quite simple:
> 1. If a noun is used in a "**defined**" or restricted context, **a determiner is required** – most commonly the **definite** article.
> 2. When a noun is used in a **non-defined** or "generalizing" context, in some cases an **indefinite article** is required, in others no article at all.

2.5.2. The definite article

How simple English is! There is only <u>one</u> definite article, and that is "**the**"; the only difficulty is knowing when to use it, and when it is not needed.

2.5.3. The indefinite article

English has **two** indefinite articles**, a** and **an.**
    a is used before nouns starting with a consonant or a semivowel,
    an is used before nouns starting with a phonetic vowel.

Examples: *a dog, a cat, an apple, an orange, an uncle*, but **a** university (because the word *university* starts with phonetic [ju:], which is not a vowel).

Indefinite articles can only be used with **count nouns**. They are used when a count noun in the singular refers to a **non-specified or non defined entity.**

Examples

> a) There's *a train* (= unspecified) coming in 5 minutes. It's *the* train (= specified) for London.
> b) Look! I can see *a hotel* over there! (= a non-identified hotel) It's *the* hotel (= specified) we're looking for!.

There is **no indefinite article in the plural**. The word "some" is occasionally referred to as a plural indefinite article, but really it is a quantifier **(like many, few, etc.).**

2.5.4. Is an article even necessary ?

Before deciding which article to use, it is first important to determine if it is indeed necessary to use any article at all. This will depend on what type of noun is being used, a **count** noun or a **non-count** noun (see § 2.3. above), and if it is a count noun, whether it is a generalisation or not.

1. Count nouns are nouns referring to items that can be counted, for example: *One car, two pens, three people, four guitars, five hotels etc.* These nouns can be used in the singular or the plural.

- **In the singular**, count nouns **must** be preceded by a determiner:

> **The** dog is happy *or* **This** dog is happy, etc.
>   *but not:* ~~Dog is happy.~~
> I'm reading **my** book *or* I'm reading **the** book ;
>   *but not:* ~~I'm reading book~~

- **In the plural**, they **may require a determiner,** depending on context (whether or not they are generalisations).

2. Non-count nouns are nouns referring to abstractions, substances or generalizations, for example: *Oxygen, health, money, heat, astronomy.*

- **In the singular**, non-count nouns do not require a determiner.
- The **plural** is even easier: non-count nouns can NOT usually be used in the plural.

2.5.5. Articles and quantifiers

Although articles are determiners, and the general rule is *"A noun is only preceded by one determiner"*, there are cases where the definite article can be preceded by a **secondary determiner** in the form of a **quantifier** or a **number.**

Examples

> a) **Some of the** tomatoes are red.
> b) **Both of the** children are very tired.
> c) **Three of the** machines were out of order.

2.6. Quantifiers

> **Definition**
> Quantifiers are a type of determiner which denote imprecise quantity. They modify nouns or pronouns. They differ from **numbers** or numerals which indicate precise quantity.
> Before pronouns, quantifiers are always followed by of.

The most common quantifiers used in English are:
some / any , much, many, a lot, a few, several, enough.

Some quantifiers, such as few or many, function as adjectives and can be qualified by an adverb of degree such as so or too. Others such as a number of function as nouns and can include or be qualified by adjectives, as in a large number of.

2.6.1. Some and any, their compounds and other neutral quantifiers

In many cases, some is used as a plural indefinite article, the plural of "a" or "an"; but more often, some implies a limited quantity, and for this reason has the value of a neutral quantifier, neither big nor small nor specific.

Some is used in affirmative statements;
it is replaced with any in negative and interrogative contexts. **Examples:**

> I've got some apples in my basket and some water in my bottle.
> I haven't got any apples in my basket, nor any water in my bottle.
> Have you got any apples in your basket? Have you got any water in your bottle?
> We had some visitors last month, but we didn't have any this month.
> Have you got any rooms free for the night of May 30th?

2.6.1.1. Special cases

Some and any used in the subject of an affirmative statement....

- As a singular subject, some implies a non-determined or non-specified entity (examples 1 - 4 below) , any implies a singular but potentially plural entity (see examples 5 - 8 below).

- Used with count nouns in the plural, some just has the function of a plural indefinite article (example 9). Any used with a plural subject has the meaning of *all*.... *if there are any* (example 10).

Examples

> Some child has left his coat on the bus.
> Some help would be appreciated. (= Will someone please help me.)
> Some famous politician once said, "To vote or not to vote?"
> Even with the best insulation, some heat always escapes.
> Any help would be appreciated.
>   (= If someone actually helped me, that would be good)
> Any accident at high speed can be fatal.
> Almost any child will say yes if you offer an ice-cream
> Any educated person knows who Shakespeare was.
> Some people are intelligent.
> Any volunteers should sign up by Friday at the latest.

2.6.1.2. *Any* or *no*

- In a **negative statement** in English, negation is normally expressed through the verb; negation can however be expressed by adding a negative value to the subject or the direct object of the sentence.
- Whenever negation is expressed in a noun phrase, the verbal negative particle *not* is replaced by the negative quantifier *no*. ▶ For more on this see § 4.5.3. Negation using nouns.

Examples

> There aren't any children in the road.
>   = There are no children in the road.
> You mustn't bring any maps with you on the expedition.
>   = You must bring no maps with you on the expedition.
> I'm not going to visit any castles in Scotland.
>   = I'm going to visit no castles in Scotland.
> Mobile phones are not allowed in the exam room.
>   = No mobile phones are allowed in the exam room.

2.6.1.3. Compound forms of *some, any* and *no*

Some any and no can be compounded with other words to form **indefinite pronouns** (see § 2.4.1.3.) ; these pronouns can be followed by a qualifying adjective. The most common compounds are

- Someone, anyone, no one
- Something, anything, nothing

- Somewhere, anywhere, nowhere

Exactly the same principles apply to these compounds, as apply to **some, any** or **no** used on their own.

Examples

Affirmation:
  There **is something** in the cupboard.
  I **put** my phone down **somewhere**.
  I've got **something important** to tell you
Negation:
  There **isn't anything** in the cupboard.
  There**'s nothing** in the cupboard.
Interrogation:
  Is there **anything** in the cupboard?
  Can you **see** my telephone **anywhere**?
  Well, can you tell us **anything new**?

2.6.1.4. *Some* in an interrogative sentence

In certain interrogative sentences (questions), **some** may be able to replace **any**.

When **some (...)** is used instead of **any (...)**, the speaker is predicting that the coming answer will be affirmative; if the same question were asked using **any**, the speaker would not be predicting any specific reply.

Examples

Is there **someone** in the room?
  (= I think there is *someone* here; am I right?)
Is there **anyone** in the room?
  (= I don't know if *anyone* is here; can someone tell me?)
Would you like **some** tea?   (An affirmative answer is expected).

2.6.1.5. With *of*: *Some of, any of, none of*

When **some, any** or **none** (but never **no**) are followed by the word **of**, the following noun must be introduced by an article or other determiner; a following **pronoun** will not of course need a determiner.

Examples

> **Some of** *the* children are eating sweets.
>   = **Some** children are eating sweets.
> Are **any of** *the* children eating sweets?
>   = Are **any** children eating sweets?
> **None of** *the* actors like working in this theatre.
>   = **No** actors like working in this theatre.
> I can answer **some of** *the* questions; he can't answer **any of them**.

Other determiners can also follow **some of / any of / none of**:

> **Some of John's** cars are very old.
> **Some of my** cars are very old.
> **Some of these** cars are very old.

Note that some of and **none of** are **never** normally followed **directly** by a noun.

- **One cannot say**: ~~Some of children~~... ~~None of animals~~ ... etc.

2.6.1.6. Other neutral quantifiers:

Several, a number of, enough   These quantifiers are dealt with under the section quantifiers of large quantity. Most commonly they express a *large or sufficiently large quantity*, often they are used with a very neutral meaning, as **synonyms of some** or **any**.

2.6.2. Large quantity quantifiers

 much, many, lots of, plenty of, numerous, a large number of, etc.

2.6.2.1 *Much* and *many (without of)*:

Much is used with non-count nouns (always in the singular); **many** is used with count nouns in the plural. (See ▶ § 2.3. the difference between count nouns and non-count nouns). Both can be qualified by adverbs of degree such as *very* or *too*.

Much and *many in affirmative statements*

In modern spoken English, **much**, and to a lesser extent **many** are **not** often used as quantifiers before nouns in <u>affirmative</u> statements, unless introduced by an intensifier, notably **so** or **too** , or followed by **of**;

Examples

> I have **many** reasons for thinking that this man is innocent
> *This is acceptable, but rather formal; most English speakers would more naturally say:*
> **I have plenty of / a lot of / ample /** reasons for thinking .....
>
> **Much** whisky is of very good quality.
> *This sentence is technically acceptable, but not probable in modern spoken English. Most people would say (and write):*
> **A lot** of whisky / **A good proportion** of whisky / **Plenty** of whisky.
>
> He has **much** money.
> *This is **not** normal English. Speakers would more naturally say:*
> He has **a lot of** money / He has **loads of** money.... etc.
>
> There is **so much** poverty in the world.
> There are **too many** people in here.
> *These examples, with **so** and **too**, are perfectly normal English.*

Remember: don't use **much** or **many** in affirmative statements, if you can avoid it. Though their use may be possible, it often sounds very formal, old-fashioned or strange in modern English.

Much and many in negative statements and questions

Much, and **many** are more commonly used in interrogative and negative contexts, and most particularly in the interrogative expressions **how much** and **how many**.

Examples

> We **don't have much** time to finish this.
> There are **not many** people who know the answer to this.
> **Did you have much** luck ?
> **How much does** this tee-shirt cost?
> **How many times do** I have to tell you not to do that ?

2.6.2.2. *Much of / many of* When is "*of*" needed ?

IMPORTANT ! If they **come before a second determiner** such as an article, a possessive or a demonstrative, or before a **pronoun**, **much** and **many must** be followed by **of**. The same principle applies to *few / few of* (see below), *some / some of*, etc.

Examples

> I can't see **many** people.
> I can't see **many of** my friends
> **Many** houses were destroyed in the war.
>   *but* **Many of the** houses were destroyed in the war.
> They didn't drink **much** beer
>   *but* They didn't drink **much of that** beer we gave them.
> **As many of** you already know, last night ....
> **Much** of what you have written is very good.
>   *This is quite acceptable in a formal context, but in spoken and less formal written style, most English-speakers would say (and write) something like:*
> **A lot of** what you have written......
> **A good deal of** what you have written.....

Much of and **many of cannot** be used <u>directly before</u> nouns.

Examples: **one cannot say:**

> ~~Much of whisky~~ is very expensive
> ~~Many of people~~ are waiting for you.

2.6.2.3. *Lots of, a lot of, plenty of, a large number of, numerous*

These expressions are all more or less synonyms. In the paragraph title above, they are arranged in order of formality, going from the most informal (**lots of**) to the most formal (**numerous**). Informal language is more appropriate in dialogue, formal language in written documents.

2.6.2.4. *Several and a number of*

These imply "*more than one, but less than a lot*". They are not usually used in negative or interrogative structures, only in affirmative statements.

Examples

> There are **several** books / **a number of** books by J.K.Rowling in our library.
> **Several** people / **A number of** people said that they'd seen the missing child.
> **Several of us** wanted to stop because the weather was so bad.

2.6.3. Small quantity quantifiers

Few, a few, little, a little, not many, not much, etc.

Except for **not much** or **not many**, these quantifiers are generally used in **affirmative statements.**

- **Little, a little, not much** are used with non-count nouns (always in the singular).
- **Few, a few, not many** are used with count nouns or pronouns in the plural.
- **Few, fewer, little** and **less** imply a quantity which is essentially small or *smaller than expected*.
- **A few** and **a little** imply small quantity, but *possibly more than expected.*

Examples

> **Few** people can speak more than three languages.
> **A few** (of the) paintings in this gallery are really good.
> There's (very) **little** point in trying to mend it. You'll never succeed!
> I've got **a little** money left; let's go and have a drink.
> There's not (too) **much** point in waiting for him to come.
> There were **fewer** people than expected.
>   (In modern English, *less* is increasingly replacing *fewer*.)

2.6.3.1. *Few* or *a few*, *little* or *a little*?

The difference between the two expressions in each phrase is purely one of **meaning**, not of **usage**.

Without the article, *few* and *little* (used respectively with count nouns and non-count nouns) have the meaning of "*not much/ not many, and possibly less than one might hope for or expect*". These expressions have a negative value to them.

With the article, *a few* and *a little* have the meaning of "*at least some, perhaps more than one might expect*". These expressions have a positive value.

Examples

> **Few** of my friends were there, so I was disappointed.
> **A few** of my friends were there, so I was quite happy.
> **A few** of them were there, so I was quite happy.
> Hurry up; there's **little** time left!
> We have **a little** time to spare, so let's stop and have a cup of coffee.

2.6.4. Neutral and relative quantifiers

Neutral quantifiers do not indicate either a large quantity or a small quantity: they are not really concerned by actual quantity, only by **relative** quantity. They are dealt with in four different groups:

>   Some and any   (see § 2.6.1 above)
>   Each and every
>   All and whole
>   Most, most of and enough

2.6.4.1. *Each* and *every*

Each and every have very similar meanings, but there are important differences of meaning and usage.

Meanings and use of each and every

- Each refers to a plural number of people or items, but it considers each person or item as an individual or dissimilar unit, it does not consider the group collectively. **Each can also be used as a pronoun**.
- Every also refers to a multiple number of people or items; but it considers these people or items as part of a similar collective group. If there are just two items or people, every may be replaced by both. **Every cannot be used as a pronoun**.

Here are some pairs of sentences that clearly illustrate the difference between each and every. In the first sentence of each pair, the speaker is implying dissimilar or individual actions: in the second of each pair, the speaker is expressing similarity of action or situation.

Examples

> Each child was reading a different book. *(dissimilar books)*
> Every child was reading a book. *(similar action)*
> You have to fill in details on each page individually. *(dissimilar pages)*
> You have to fill in details on every page. *(similar action)*
> We go on holiday to a different place each summer. *(dissimilar destinations)*
> We go on holiday to Brighton every summer. *(similar action)*
> He makes a different mistake each time. *(dissimilar action)*
> He makes the same mistake every time. *(similar action)*

Sometimes it is important to distinguish between **each** and **every**; in other cases, this distinction is not important, and the user can choose either word.

Usage

Both *each* and *every* are **singular** quantifiers. When they determine the subject of a sentence, they normally (but not always) require a verb in the singular.

Examples

> Each member of the committee **was** allowed to speak once.
> Each of us was allowed to speak for five minutes
> Every cloud **has** a silver lining.
> Each day **is** different.
> Every person I know **has** seen the film.

Particular uses of each

Each as a quantifier can be used with three different structures.

- Structure 1 : **each** + singular noun
- Structure 2 : **each + of** + plural noun / pronoun
- Structure 3 : Plural noun / pronoun + **each**

Take care! **Singular or plural ?**

When *each* is used in the *subject* of a sentence:

- The verb is in the **singular** if **each** comes before the noun or pronoun (**structures 1** and **2**).
- The verb is in the **plural** if **each** follows the noun or pronoun that it determines **(structure 3).** When **each** follows a noun or **pronoun**, it may do so directly, or else be placed between the auxiliary and the verb

Examples

> Structure 1. Each child **was** reading a book.
> Structure 2. Each of the children **was** reading a book.
>   Each of us **has** a different answer.
> Structure 3. The children **were** each reading a book.
>   or The children each **were** reading a book.
>   We each **have** provided a different answer.
>   We **have** each provided a different answer.

2.6.4.2. All and whole

All and **whole** express **totality** or **completeness**.

Sometimes one can choose either of them; but there are major differences in their usage, and *all* and *whole* are not always interchangeable.

- **All** can refer to singular nouns or pronouns, or to plural nouns or pronouns.
- **Whole** is essentially used with nouns in the singular. It is occasionally used as a descriptive adjective with nouns in the plural, and cannot normally be used with pronouns.

1. All with singular nouns.

There are three structures possible, as in these examples:

- **All day / all the time / all of the day**

Usually a determiner is required, but **of** is not required, and its use depends on context or choice. If **all of** is used with a singular noun, it <u>must</u> be followed by a determiner, as in **all of the day,** not ~~all of day.~~

Determiners that can be used in this structure are **the**, demonstrative adjectives (**this, that**), possessive adjectives (**my, your,** etc.), possessive forms of the noun (**Peter's, the man's,** etc.).

When the phrase with **all** is the **subject** of a statement, the verb is normally in the singular – unless the noun in the group is a collective noun referring to multiple people, such as team, committee, school, or family, when the verb is normally in the plural (examples 3, 4 and 5).

Examples

1. **All** the factory was on fire.
2. **All** (of) my collection of old books has been stolen.
3. **All** the school know that the principal has won the lottery.
    or **All** the school knows that the principal has won the lottery.
4. **All** my family are coming to dinner tomorrow.
    All my family is coming to dinner tomorrow. sounds improbable
5. **All** the President's team are standing for re-election.
6. **All** (of) this rubbish must be cleared up at once!
7. I want you to clear up **all** (of) this rubbish.
8. **Not all** art is valuable. *Take care! This means* "Some art is not valuable": *it does not mean* " **No** works of art are valuable".

2. *All* with *plural nouns*

Plural nouns are by definition count nouns, so the situation is less complicated. There are three structures, as in these examples
- *All children / all the children / all of the children :*

Whether to use a determiner or not depends on the context, and follows exactly the normal rules for count nouns in the plural. It depends if the noun is being used as an **open generalisation** (no determiner), examples 1 - 5, or as a **limited generalisation** (with determiner), examples 6 - 8.

Examples

1. **All** diamonds are valuable
2. **All** fish live in water.
3. I like **all** kinds of music.
4. He gave **all** sorts of excuses for being late.
5. **All** multinational companies have operations in several countries.
6. **All (of) the** diamonds in this shop are very valuable.
7. **All (of) the** fish that I've eaten have been very tasty .
8. I like **all (of) the** music that you play on your violin.

3. *Whole*

Whole as a **quantifier** can only be used with **singular** nouns, either singular count nouns or singular non-count nouns. It is used exactly like a normal adjective, on the models:
- { the + **whole** (+of + determiner) + noun}.
- { the + **whole** (+of + determiner) + adjective +noun}.

Whole has a similar meaning to *all,* though the structures are different.

However, by using *the whole* one stresses the **unity** of an entity, not its multiple components. Thus when the subject of a sentence is a collective noun implying multiple people , such as *team, committee, school,* or *family*, qualified by **whole**, the verb is most often in the singular (contrast this with *all*, above).

Examples with whole

You will tell the truth, the **whole** truth, and nothing but the truth.
This **whole** (of the) story has been made up.
We'll have to repaint the **whole** (of the) room.
There was a **whole** complicated dossier to fill in.
The **whole** (of the) English team was welcomed by the Queen.

4. *Note*: *Whole* and place names:

The structure {the + **whole** + noun} is **not** used with place names that do not **already** contain an article, notably the names of countries. One can say *the whole United States,* but one **cannot** say *the whole England*: one can say *the **whole of** England.*

Examples:

> OK   The virus caused thousands of deaths throughout **the whole of the** United States.
> OK   The virus caused thousands of deaths throughout **the whole** United States.
> OK   **The whole of** London was put on alert.
> Not OK   ~~The whole London~~ was put on alert.

2.6.4.3. *Most, most of* and *enough*

There are a couple of common quantifiers that express relative or proportional quantity.

Most / most of

These imply *more than half of, a majority of,* or *almost all.* They **do not** mean the same as *many / many of* .

Enough

Enough implies a *sufficient quantity*; it is used in affirmations, negations and questions.

> I've done **enough** work for one day.
> There were **enough** strong men to move the fallen tree.
> We can get tickets for the concert, I've got **enough** money now.
> Have you got **enough** money for the tickets?
> No, I haven't got **enough**.

Take care !   *Do not confuse....*

enough as a quantifier adjective preceding a noun, as in
> *I've done enough work for one day.*

with *enough* as an intensifier following an adjective, as in:
> *That's good enough for me.*

2.6.5. Take care: Quantifiers with of...

Much of, many of, few of, a little of, plenty of, lots of, some of, a number of, none of, enough of, several of, etc.

Of is **always** required between a quantifier and a pronoun, as in:

> Most of us were very worried about the pandemic.
> As for the spectators, lots of them just wanted to go home.

Before nouns, there is a choice of two possible structures: With most determiners the choice is between
- either {quantifier + noun}
- or {quantifier + of + determiner + noun}

BUT With a few quantifiers, such as a lot, a few, plenty, of is **always** required, whether there is a determiner or not.

The rule....	... applies to
You can use *either* quantifier + noun, *or* quantifier + of + determiner + noun	all, each, some, many, much, (a) few, (a) little, none, several, enough,
Of is always required, with or without a determiner	plenty of, a lot of, lots of, a number of, a couple of, a handful of, etc.

Here are a few examples; most are right, some are wrong.

> OK Some of the people are right some of the time, but all of the people cannot be right all of the time.
> Not OK ~~Some of people~~ are right ~~some of time~~, ~~but all of people~~ cannot be right ~~all of time~~.
> OK Plenty of supporters came to the match.
> OK Plenty of the supporters came to the match.
> Not OK ~~Plenty supporters~~ came to the match.
> OK Several of the players were sent off.
> OK Several players were sent off.
> Not OK ~~Several of players~~ were sent off.
> OK I'd like a few of these apples, please.
> OK I'd like a few of your apples, please.
> Not OK ~~I'd like a few of apples, please.~~
> Not OK ~~I'd like few of apples, please.~~

2.7. Numbers

2.7.1. Cardinal numbers

Cardinal numbers are the numbers that we use for counting or designating quantity: English-speakers use them every day - *one two three four* etc.

Grammatical functions

Cardinal numbers can be used as **determiners** or **numeral adjectives** in front of nouns, or else as **indefinite pronouns**. (see § 2.4.1.3.)

Examples

> I ordered **six** boxes, but I've only received **three**.
> **Twenty-five** runners started the race, but only **eleven** finished.

From 0 to 100 - From zero to a hundred

The number **0** is variously expressed as **nought** (in British English) or **zero** (in all forms of English): in the middle of a series of digits, it may also be pronounced "**oh**". Everyone has heard of James Bond, also known as **007**. That is pronounced "**double-oh-seven**" or "**oh-oh-seven**", but never "*nought-nought-seven*" nor "*zero-zero-seven*".

Here are the important cardinal numbers between one and a hundred, which can serve as models for other numbers.

1	one	11	eleven	21	twenty-one
2	two	12	twelve	22	twenty-two
3	three	13	thirteen	30	thirty
4	four	14	fourteen	40	forty
5	five	15	fifteen	50	fifty
6	six	16	sixteen	60	sixty
7	seven	17	seventeen	70	seventy
8	eight	18	eighteen	80	eighty
9	nine	19	nineteen	90	ninety
10	ten	20	twenty	100	a hundred

TAKE CARE ! Watch out for spelling: **fourteen** but **forty**.

Numbers from 101 to 999 - three-digit numbers

> **Important:** the examples and rules below illustrate **British** usage.
> In the **USA**, the word *and* is normally omitted. A hyphen (-) is normally used in numbers between 21 and 99, whether these stand alone or are part of a larger number.

From the following examples, all other three-digit numbers in English can be formed.

101	a hundred and one	365	three hundred and sixty-five
111	a hundred and eleven	480	four hundred and eighty
121	a hundred and twenty-one	545	five hundred and forty-five
133	a hundred and thirty-three	644	six hundred and forty-four
257	two hundred and fifty-seven	799	seven hundred and ninety-nine

Notes:

The word **hundred**, except as a round number (a number ending in **00**), is always followed by "**and**", both in spoken English and in written English when numbers are written out as words.

The word **hundred** never takes an "**s**" as part of a cardinal number.
For numbers between 100 and 199, one normally says "**a hundred**" and not "**one hundred**".
The expression **one hundred** is used only to put emphasis on the figure **one** (i.e. *one*, not *two* nor *three*), or to stress the word.

Example:

I counted **one** hundred and twenty planes   (and not 220 nor 320).

Hundreds in the plural

The words **hundred, thousand** and **million** never take an **s** in the plural as cardinal numbers (which are a form of adjective). They only take an **s** when used as nouns designating an **imprecise quantity** of **hundreds** or **thousands**, etc., followed by *of* ...

Examples

> There are hundreds of ducks on the lake.
>
> Thousands of people crammed into the stadium.

These sentences do not say *how many* hundreds nor *how many* thousands: the "s" is the only mark of plurality.

Numbers from 1000 to 1,000,000

- Apart from round numbers (numbers ending in 00) numbers above 1000 are normally written in **figures**, not in words. *They are written in words here as a means to show how they are used in spoken English.*

1000	a thousand	4656	four thousand six hundred and fifty-six
1001	a thousand and one	10,000	ten thousand
1086	one thousand and eighty-six	10,148	ten thousand one hundred and forty-eight
1147	one thousand one hundred and forty-seven	65,423	sixty-five thousand four hundred and twenty-three
1201	one thousand two hundred and one	100,000	A hundred thousand
3600	three thousand six hundred	699,482	Six hundred and ninety-nine thousand four hundred and eighty-two

> **Reminder:** these examples and rules reflect usage in British English. In the USA, the word *and* is usually omitted.

- **After 1000**, if the word "**hundred**" does not occur in the number, it is the word **thousand** which is followed by **and**.
- **Apart from round numbers** (1000, 7000 etc.) there will always be an **and** somewhere in the number.
- The word **hundred** is always followed by "**and**" once it is followed by another digit, and *even if it occurs more than once* in the number.
- Whether writing in figures or in words, with numbers of more than four digits it is normal to put a **comma** every three digits. The comma is optional with four-digit numbers.

Examples;
1018 = One thousand **and** eighteen
    (or in US English: One thousand eighteen)
43,003 = forty-three thousand **and** three
56,100 = fifty-six thousand one hundred
25,864 = Twenty-five thousand eight hundred **and** sixty-four
654,122 = Six hundred **and** fifty-four thousand, one hundred **and** twenty-two

- In numbers **from 1100 to 1199**, the figure **1** is usually pronounced in full, **one** and not **a,** before the words **thousand** and **hundred.**
- **Four-digit numbers below 2000** (and rarely above) may sometimes also be expressed starting with "**eleven hundred**", "twelve hundred", etc. This is the normal way of expressing the **year** in dates.

Examples

1618 = One thousand six hundred and eighteen, *or*
The year sixteen hundred and eighteen

Numbers greater than a million

The same principles apply. The number simply starts with a quantity of millions (or billions) for example *One million...*or *Twenty-five million...* or *Eight hundred and twenty million...*or *two billion*

Examples

1,002,018 = One million two thousand and eighteen
1,001,116 = One million one thousand one hundred and sixteen.
736,654,121 = Seven hundred and thirty-six million, six hundred and fifty-four thousand, one hundred and twenty-one

The word **hundred** is always followed by "**and**" unless it is round (with "00"), no matter how often it occurs in the number.

2.7.2. Ordinal numbers

Numerical adjectives of order

Ordinals **are words like** *first, second, third.....*

They are adjectives formed from cardinal numbers. They are used to indicate the position of an entity in a stated or implied series.

In common usage, written as figures, they are formed by a number followed by an abbreviated ending corresponding to the ending of the written word. In most cases the ending is **th**; but this is not always the case . Ordinals derived from cardinals in **–y** (such as **twenty**) end in **–ieth**.

Ordinals are also used to express fractions and dates. In the case of fractions, the endings are not written when the fractions are expressed in figures.

From 1st to 100th

Here are the main ordinals in English, up to **hundredth**; from these examples all others can be formed.

1st	first	11th	eleventh	21st	twenty-first
2nd	second	12th	twelve	22nd	twenty-second
3rd	third	13th	thirteenth	33rd	thirty-third
4th	fourth	14th	fourteenth	44th	forty-fourth
5th	fifth	15th	fifteenth	50th	fiftieth
6th	sixth	16th	sixteenth	60th	sixtieth
7th	seventh	17th	seventeenth	71st	seventy-first
8th	eighth	18th	eighteenth	82nd	eighty-second
9th	ninth	19th	nineteenth	99th	ninety-ninth
10th	tenth	20th	twentieth	100th	a hundredth

Ordinals after 100th

From these examples you can see how all ordinals are formed.

101st	hundred and first	365th	three hundred and sixty-fifth
111th	hundred and eleventh	500th	five hundredth
121st	hundred and twenty first	545th	five hundred and forty-fifth
133rd	hundred and thirty-third	644th	six hundred and forty-fourth
257th	two hundred and fifty-seventh	999th	nine hundred and ninety nine
302nd	three hundred and second	1250th	one thousand two hundred and fiftieth

Note: ordinals can be preceded by a range of different articles or determiners

Examples

> **The** first anniversary - the 1st anniversary
> **My** twenty-first birthday - My 21st birthday
> **Three** hundredths of a second - 3/100 of a second.
> **My** hundred and second attempt - My 102nd attempt.
> **The US** Hundred and first Airborne division - The US 101st Airborne division
> You are **our** millionth visitor. You are our 1,000,000th visitor

Other points to note:

Translating numbers into other languages.

The basic rule is simple: translate using words when the original number is written in words, translate using figures when the original uses figures.

Examples

> The **three** musketeers = Les **trois** mousquetaires.
> My **21st** birthday - Mein **21.** Geburtstag.
> **Three hundredths** of a second - **Tres centésimas** de segundo
> His **203rd** attempt - Zijn **203** poging.
> The US **Hundred and first** Airborne division - **La cent-unième** division US aeroportée.

2.7.3. Fractions & decimals

1. Fractions

Fractions, which express quantities less than one, should not cause many problems for students of English, once they have understood how they are formed.

Except for the most common fractions, ¼ ½ and ¾, fractions are made up of a cardinal number (**one, two, three** etc.) followed by an **ordinal**, usually in the plural (**thirds, fifths, sixths** etc.) Here are the most common fractions in English, and a few others as random examples.

1/4	a quarter (occasionally a fourth)	3/16	three sixteenths
1/2	a half	1/32	one thirty-second
3/4	three quarters	7/9	seven ninths
1/3	a third	1/100	a hundredth or one hundredth
2/3	two thirds	12/100	twelve hundredths
3/8	three eighths	21/1000	twenty-one thousandths

Fractions are used in all styles of language, including scientific and technical English. In particular, North Americans, notably people in the USA, have not fully adopted the decimal system like most of the rest of the world, and still use non-metric measurements such as **feet** and **inches**.... and fractions of these.

Examples

> **Half** a pint of beer
> **A quarter** of a second
> **Three quarters** of a mile
> **Three fifths** of the contents of the bottle
> A thickness of **one thirty-second** of an inch
> A tolerance of **six thousandths** of a millimetre.

2 Decimals

Decimals are regularly used in everyday English, but more specifically in scientific and technical English, in order to indicate with precision quantities that are not a complete number. They are not difficult to use.

After the **decimal point** figures are expressed digit by digit. The words **hundred** and **thousand** are never used after the decimal point.

Note that the decimal **point** is precisely that; a **point**, not a comma. **Before** a decimal point, for a quantity less than 1, one normally begins (British English) **nought point** ... or (all forms of English) **zero point** .... But **after** the decimal point, the **0** is expressed as "**oh**" or "**nought**" or "**zero**".

0.25	point two five *or* nought point two five, *or* zero point two five	8.56	eight point five six
0.5	point five, *or* nought point five, *or* zero point five	12.15	twelve point one five
0.75	point seven five, *or* nought point seven five *or* zero point seven five	17.806	seventeen point eight oh six
0.333	point three three three, *or* nought point three three three, *or* zero point three three three	384.63	three hundred and eighty-four point six three
0.6405	nought point six four oh five *or* zero point six four zero five	40.004	Forty point oh oh four *or* Forty point nought nought four, *or* Forty point zero zero four
1.5	one point five	117.87659	one hundred and seventeen point eight seven six five nine

Important; except on very rare occasions, figures with decimals are never written out in **words**, but always written in **figures**. On this page, examples are expressed in words as a representation of the way they are expressed in spoken English.

Examples

Written; It was 0.2445 mm thick.
  Oral; It was nought point two four four five millimetres thick.
Written; The long side measures 6.652 in.
  Oral; The long side measures six point six five two inches.
Written; The solar vehicle reached a record speed of 131.68 m.p.h.
  Oral; The solar vehicle reached a record speed of a hundred and thirty-one point six eight miles an hour (or miles per hour).

2.8. Possession

*Possessive structures in English - use of *of* and *'s**

There is no absolute rule to tell you whether you need to use, or can use, a possessive form with "**of**", on one with "**'s**". The commonly repeated "rule" that you can "only use 's with people" is quite wrong. It is a very broad generalisation, and there are lots of exceptions. Besides, there are a lot of cases where, even with people, you cannot use **'s**.

2.8.1. Animates: human possessors, or assimilated:

2.8.1.1.

In cases of true possession: **'s** is normal. In many cases it will be essential.

A1 The lady's car wouldn't start.
A2 The dog's ball was red..

With qualities, attributes or actions: **'s** is common.

A3 Madonna's reputation is international.
A4 The dog's name was Jackson.
A5 The Queen's arrival was delayed.

These can also be easily expressed using **of**.

A31 The reputation of Madonna is international.
A41 The name of the dog was Jackson.

There is a **difference in emphasis** between the two alternatives: examples:

- A3-A5 emphasize the possessor,
- A31 and A41 emphasize the quality or attribute.

In A5, the "possessor" is the subject of the verbal noun (*arrival*) following it
Situations in which there is no choice:
Sometimes, even though both forms are theoretically possible, the **structure** of a sentence will determine the choice of expression, as a word may **have to** stand next to other words qualifying it: for example:

A32 The reputation of Madonna, the American singer, is international

We can **NOT** say:

A32X ** ~~Madonna's reputation, the American singer, is international.~~ **

Examples A1 and A2 must be rephrased using "of" if this is structurally **essential**:

> A 11 The car of the lady I had lunch with wouldn't start
> Clearly, the other theoretical option gives the wrong meaning!
>   A 11x ~~**The lady's car I had lunch with wouldn't start.**~~

2.8.1.2. Possessive adjectives:

There is no choice when possession is indicated by a possessive adjective, such as *his, my, your,* etc.

> A61   Your loss is my gain.
> A62   I took my brother to see our grandfather.
>   A 62x ~~I took the brother of me to see the grandfather of us.~~

2.8.1.3. Relating a part to a whole (animates)

Use of "of" is **obligatory** when expressing the relation of **a proportion to a composite whole.**

> A71   the **rest of the people**,
> A72   the **majority of voters.**
> A73   a **quarter of the committee**

We can NOT say:

> A71x: ~~the people's rest,~~
> A72x: ~~the voters' majority~~
> A73x: ~~the committee's quarter~~

Of and **'s** are both possible (depending on sentence structure) when expressing the relation of **a part** to **a unitary** (single) **whole**.

> A8 The **man's arm** was broken, *or*
> A81 The **arm of the man** was broken

2.8.1.4 : Singular **nouns ending in** *s*. There are two possible ways to use these in the **'s** possessive form. Compare two examples: **Saint James's Park** is a park in London, but **Saint James' Park** is a famous football stadium in Newcastle. Both names are correct.

2.8.2. Inanimate possessors

For qualities, attributes, actions, or parts: **Of** is the **usual** structure, but **'s** may be possible;

The unusual "'s" form can be used with <u>some familiar</u> nouns for stress, or for reasons of sentence structure.

B1	The cost of the operation was enormous.
B2	The condition of the goods we received was not very satisfactory.
B3	The launch of the new book was very successful.
B31	The new **book's** launch was very successful.
B4	Where's the lid of the saucepan?
B5	The front end of the car was smashed up.
B51	The **car's** front end was smashed up.
B6	The departure of the train was delayed for an hour.
B61	The **train's** departure was delayed for an hour.

In examples B3 and B6, where the attribute that is "possessed" is a verbal noun, the sentence could be rephrased using subject and verb instead of the possessive structures.

B32	The **new book was launched** very successfully (subj. + passive verb).
B62	The **train departed** an hour later than planned (subj. + active verb).

2.8.2.1. Relating a part to a whole (inanimates) or a group to its constituents

The **of** form is normally obligatory when expressing the relation of a **part** to a **whole** (or **a whole** to its **parts**) when the part has no meaning except in relation to the whole.

B7	The **top of** the **stairs**.
	(i.e. the word **top** is meaningless without reference to **stairs**.)
B8	The **back of** the **building**
B9	The **middle of** the **report**

The same is usually true when expressing the relation of a **unit** to a **group** (or **a group** to **its units**) when the group is defined by the units of which it is composed.

B10	A **collection of paintings**
B11	A **group of trees**

We can **NOT** say:

B71x:	~~the stairs' top~~.
B81x:	~~the building's back.~~
B101x	~~A paintings' collection~~

However there sometimes **is a choice** when the **part** is expressed as adjective+noun, or when the **part** is more important in the phrase than the whole (B 13, B131),

B12	The **top floor** of the building
B121	The building's **top floor**
B 13	The **roof** of the building was on fire
B 131	The building's **roof** was on fire.

2.8.2.2. Complemental noun groups

Of is essential, except in a few specific cases.

C1	The theory of relativity *NOT:* ~~the relativity's theory~~
C2	The Department of Linguistics *NOT:* ~~the Linguistics's department~~

Complemental noun groups can often be rephrased as **compounds**, without **'s**:

C11	the relativity theory
C21	the Linguistics Department

2.9. Adjectives

An **adjective** is a word that **defines, qualifies or modifies** the meaning of a **noun**, or more rarely of a **pronoun**. It expresses a quality or attribute of the word it qualifies. There are two main categories of adjectives: **determining** adjectives, and **descriptive** adjectives, which can be either **qualifying** adjectives or **classifying** adjectives.

2.9.1. Determining adjectives

Also called **limiting** adjectives, determining adjectives are words that are generally classed in the family of **determiners**, and are dealt with elsewhere: there is a limited number of these words. They are notably possessive adjectives (such as *my, their*), numerals and quantifiers (such as *one, two, three, every, many*), demonstrative adjectives (such as *this* or *that*), interrogative adjectives (such as *which*). For information on the use of these determining adjectives, consult the appropriate paragraphs.

2.9.2. Descriptive adjectives: qualifying or classifying

When we talk of **adjectives**, what we generally tend to think of are "**descriptive adjectives**". These are adjectives such as *big, English, wonderful*, words that describe the permanent or perceived qualities of a noun; their number is unlimited. New descriptive adjectives enter the language every day, often in the fertile world of slang.

There are two categories of descriptive adjectives;

- **qualifying or qualificative adjectives**, such as *big, nice, complicated* which express the passing or perceived qualities of a noun, and
- **classifying adjectives** (including **absolute** adjectives) such as *married, second, hydraulic, unique, dead* which express permanent qualities or absolutes.

Qualifying adjectives are "**gradable**", i.e. it is possible to graduate their intensity, by the addition of an adverb of degree, such as *very, quite, enough*; most qualifying adjectives can also be put into comparative or superlative forms (*big, bigger, biggest*).

Classifying adjectives cannot normally be graded: a person is either *married* or not, or *dead* or not; he or she cannot be "*very married*", nor "*more dead*" than another person, at least not under normal usage of the words.

That being said, many adjectives can be used *either* as qualifying adjectives, *or* as classifying adjectives, depending on the context. Take the example of the adjective *old*.

Examples

My car is very **old.** (qualifying, with a noun)
He is **old.** (qualifying, with a pronoun)
The **old** computer was much quieter than the **new** model. (classifying)

In the first two examples above, *old* is a perceived quality, and therefore gradable, in the third *old* has an absolute value, with the meaning of *former* or *previous*.

See gradation and comparison of adjectives below.

2.9.3. Use of adjectives: attributive or predicative

Adjectives are used in two main ways; they can either be **attributive** or they can be **predicative**.

2.9.3.1. *Attributive adjectives:*

This is the most common use of adjectives, standing next to a noun in a noun phrase. In English, simple and complex adjectives almost always come **before** the noun.

Examples

The **big metal** box
My **dear old** grandfather.
A very **modern plastic** dish.
An easily **recognisable** face.
A **pink and green** dress
A **not-too-infrequent** event.

Exceptions: adjectives that follow *nouns or pronouns. (postpositive adjectives)*

There are only a very small number of exceptions,
a) A few adjectives such as *concerned involved, present* and *responsible*, which have a particular meaning when they come after a noun.
b) Some adjectives, notably participles, which can follow a noun when they stand as the contraction of an unexpressed relative clause. (examples 3 & 4)

c) Adjectives that qualify pronouns (examples 5 & 6) must follow.
d) Adjectives of dimension or duration, such as *old* and *tall,* follow the noun in some cases, notably when used predicatively. (ex. 7 & 8)
e) The other important case when an adjective will follow a noun is when the adjective is postmodified by a prepositional phrase. (examples 9 & 10)

Examples

1. All the people **concerned** were told to leave the room.
2. The children **present** did not like the show. (=The children *who were present* ....)
3. He's the last man **standing**.
4. There are only three cakes **left**.
5. I want to give you something **special.**
6. That would be quite understandable to anyone **intelligent**.
7. The man is **seven feet tall** and I'm **20 years old**.
8. There's a **metre deep** hole in the road, and it's **six metres long.**
9. I bought all the bottles left in the shop.
10. He was a man proud of his success

For details on the ordering of adjectives within a noun group, see adjective order below.

2.9.3.2. Predicative adjectives

Adjectives are said to be **predicative** when they are used as the complement of the verb **to be,** or other similar verbs such as *get, become, grow,* as in these examples.

The result was **magnificent**.
My girlfriend is **beautiful**.
The weather is getting **colder**.
I grew **fonder** of London after living there for a month.

2.9.4. Adjectives in the plural

In English, adjectives **never** take a plural inflexion **(s)** whether they are used attributively or predicatively, for example.

Twelve **good** men.... ***Never*** Twelve ~~goods~~ men

The same rule applies to some **adjectives used as nouns.**

We talk about **the poor**, or **the living**, or **the wounded**. We cannot say ~~the poors~~ or ~~the livings~~, or ~~the woundeds~~.

Example

The **injured** and **the** dead were evacuated by ambulance.

On the other hand, with **colours**, specially when referring to teams, adjectives used as nouns do take a plural **s**.

Example

The final is between **the reds** and **the blues**.

2.9.5. Formation of adjectives

Many adjectives are lexical words in their own right, i.e. they exist independently of any other word, or are the root word of a word family. For example *good, bad, ugly*. Other adjectives are inflected forms of other words, derived notably from verbs. For example *charming, lost*. Other adjectives can be formed from nouns, for example *beautiful* (from *beauty*) or *motionless* (from *motion*), or even from other adjectives (for example *yellowish*).

One of the beauties of the English language is the simplicity with which words can be formed from other words: all that is needed is to add the appropriate prefix or suffix, and a new word is made. Here are some examples.

Unthinkable, doable, mendable, possible, plausible - with *-able* or *-ible*
Careless, fruitless, homeless, motionless - with *less*
Beautiful, hopeful, wonderful, awful, blissful - with *ful*
Soggy, foggy, lazy, stormy, skinny, bloody, - with *-y*
Smallish, greenish, darkish, - with *-ish*
Distinguished, bored, displaced, contented, squared - with *-ed*
Challenging, alarming, amazing, exciting - with *-ing*

2.9.6. Comparison of adjectives

Many qualifying adjectives can be used in a **comparative** or a **superlative** form. In most cases, the comparative form of an adjective is made with the word *more*, and the superlative form with the word *most*.

But with most common short monosyllabic adjectives, and some two-syllable adjectives, the comparative is made by adding the ending *-er*, and the superlative with the ending *-est*. There are two common adjectives with irregular comparative and superlative forms: *good, better, best*, and *bad, worse, worst*.

Examples

> **Careful**, more careful, most careful **Difficult**, more difficult, most difficult
> **Certain**, more certain, most certain **Hard**, harder, hardest, **Old**, older, oldest, **Black**, blacker, blackest, **Clever**, cleverer, cleverest
> **Large**, larger, largest (just add *-r* and *-st* to adjectives ending in e)
> **Big**, bigger, biggest, **hot**, hotter, hottest - Note that final **p t k b d g n** & **m**, are doubled when standing *alone after a short vowel.*
> **Hard**, harder, **warm** warmer, **quiet** quieter - Note that final **p t k b d g n** & **m**, are **not** doubled when *following another consonant or a long vowel or diphthong.*
> **Pretty**, prettier, prettiest , **heavy**, heavier, heaviest
> Adjectives ending in **y** have inflected forms in **-ier** and **-iest**.

2.9.7. Gradation of adjectives - adverbs of degree

Qualifying adjectives can be graded by **adverbs of degree** or of intensity, and by some other adverbs. Common adverbs of intensity include: *quite, rather, fairly, very, extremely, highly, pretty, (all) that, too* .

These adverbs come before the adjective. But note the following points:

- **Enough**: qualifying an adjective, *enough* comes, exceptionally, after the word it qualifies (examples 6 and 7). (Qualifying a noun, *enough* comes before the word it qualifies).

- **Rather** and **quite**: used attributively, *quite* and *rather* can either follow the article, or come before the article: i.e. we can choose between *a rather good book* and *rather a good book*, or *quite a nice guy* and *a quite nice guy*. With **rather**, the choice is generally open, with **quite** it is more usual to say *quite a* than *a quite*.

- **That**, and sometimes **this**, meaning *to such a degree,* can be used to qualify a predicative adjective (examples 8 & 9). Like **too** and **so**, they can also precede an attributive adjective (ex. 10 & 11), but in this case the adjective must be followed by **a (an)** before a singular count noun. They can also be used before quantifiers such as *much, many* or *few* (ex. 12)

Adjectives that are in the comparative form can be modified by intensifiers such as *much, far* and sometimes by adverbs of degree (examples 13). Some kinds of adjectives, notably participles, can be modified by a wide range of adverbs (examples 14 and 15).

> 1. I'm *quite certain* I left my hat in the car.
> 2. This is a *rather good* film OR this *is rather a good* film.

3. It's very clear that you have read the book already.
4. This is a highly complicated situation to be in.
5. This situation is pretty complicated.
6. OK, that was a clear enough reply.
7. Is the door wide enough to get through ?
8. I really don't think that the answer was (all) that easy to follow.
9. If it's that expensive, I can't afford it.
10. If it's that simple a solution, then where is the problem?
11. This is so good a book that I can't put it down!
12. That much money will buy you quite a lot.
13. This was much better than last time. It's rather better than I expected.
14. They are a newly married couple.
15. He made a carefully worded statement.

Classifying adjectives can not normally be graded, though there are some circumstances where grading is possible. Compare the three examples below using the classifying adjective *electric*. Normally something is *electric* or it is *not electric*; it can't be *very electric* nor *quite electric*...... However it can be *mainly electric*.

Examples

OK: This new car is electric.
Not OK: ~~This new car is **very** electric.~~
OK. This new hybrid car is **mainly** electric.

2.9.8. The order of adjectives

How is it that native English speakers naturally place adjectives (and secondary nouns acting as adjectives) in the "correct" order when writing or speaking? Very few native English speakers have ever learnt, or even thought of, the rules that determine the order in which adjectives are placed. This obviously means that the rules are a) very basic and intuitive, and b) very few in number. More than rules, they are conventions.

Adjectives are placed in English according to their nature or type. There are **three groups** of adjectives, defining the qualities of a noun:

> **A. Articles & accessories**, relative or perceived circumstantial qualities.
> At the start of group **A** come **A**rticles and determiners
> **B. B**asic, permanent but circumstantial qualities
> **C. C**lassifying adjectives, innate or **fundamental permanent qualities**

And of course, they will be placed in the natural order **ABC**, with **the most fundamental adjectives coming closest to the noun, i.e. last.** Each **group** contains different types of adjectives, which may (or may not) require a specific sequence.

This is illustrated in the following table:

Group A	Group B	Group C	Noun
Articles and accessories	Basic	Classifying	
Article or determiner > Perceived quality, > Size, weight, age etc.	Colour > Nationality > Gender (sometimes gender before nationality)	Permanent quality > substance (often a secondary noun)	
An attractive ancient	British	copper	necklace
My first big	green	rubber	ball
His five old	American		cousins.
	British female		voters
Magnificent old	American	Ford	automobile.
Memorable	French	skiing	holiday
Dangerous and useless		chemical	experiment
Nice fresh	red Spanish		tomatoes

Important! When two group A adjectives of similar nature qualify the same noun, they **may** be linked by *and*. However *and* is **never** required to link adjectives from different groups.

If two adjectives before a **plural** noun are joined by *and*, the phrase may imply two different categories, though a certain ambiguity will often remain, as in: *Attractive and valuable old books can be bought online.*

3 Other parts of speech

3.1. Adverbs

3.1.1. Two families of adverb

There are two main families of adverb:

16. Adverbs related to or derived from adjectives or prepositions.
17. Adverbs unrelated to adjectives or prepositions.

Adverbs from either category may fulfil identical functions in the sentence. Each category includes adverbs of four main types: time, place, manner and degree.

Category 1:

1. **Time:** (duration, sequence): presently, previously, fast
2. **Place:** (position or direction): locally, closely, upwards, nearby
3. **Manner:** Quickly, easily, consequently
4. **Degree:** Extremely, generally, highly, nearly

Category 2:

1. **Time:** (duration, sequence): already, soon, tomorrow, next
2. **Place:** (position or direction): Here, there, somewhere, away
3. **Manner:** too, thus, therefore
4. **Degree:** very, quite

Particular points : Adverbs of degree:

Some adverbs of **degree** are used in particular ways. See § 2.9.7. above. Gradation of adjectives.

3.1.1.1. Function of adverbs

Whereas adjectives are used to qualify a noun, **adverbs** are used to qualify a verb, an adjective, or another adverb. Some adverbs - called "sentence adverbs" - can also qualify a whole sentence (see § 3.1.4. below).

3.1.2. Adverbs related to adjectives

Most adverbs in English are related to adjectives; for example *high* (adjective) and *highly* (adverb).

Adjectives	Adverbs	
Qualifying a noun	qualifying a verb	qualifying an adjective
A **high** mountain	I think **highly** of you	That is **highly** improbable
A **real** surprise	He **really** likes you	You are **really** nice.
A **fast** train	It went very **fast**	This is a **fast** moving situation.
In **actual** fact	I **actually** laughed	
A **bitter** disappointment	I **bitterly** regret saying that.	A **bitterly** cold day

3.1.2.1 Formation of adverbs

As the examples above show, many adverbs are formed by adding the ending **-ly** to an adjective. Adverbs can be formed from many adjectives in this manner; that includes many participles.

Examples: (adjective / adverb) new / newly, continuous / continuously, recent / recently,
Adjectives ending in *-ful* form adverbs ending in *-fully*: careful / carefully,
Adjectives ending in *-y* form adverbs ending in *-ily*: happy / happily,

Participial adjectives:
Surprising / surprisingly, disgusting / disgustingly, decided / decidedly

There are a few exceptions to this principle.

A few adverbs (and related adjectives) are formed by adding the endings **-ward(s), -ways** or **-wise** to nouns or prepositions.

> clockwise , anti-clockwise, counter-clockwise, sideways, sidewards, forwards, inwards, upwards, skywards etc.

Words in *-wise* can share the same form as adverbs or adjectives; adverbs ending in *-wards* normally lose the final **s** when used as adjectives.

> A clockwise rotation, a sideways movement
> ….in an upward(s) direction, a forward motion

Finally, note that the normal adverb corresponding to the adjective **good** is **well**, not goodly.

3.1.2.2. Adjectives and adverbs with *identical forms*

Here are the eight most common adjective/adverb pairs that share identical forms:

Adjectives	Adverbs	Notes:
A **fast** train	It went very **fast**	
A **hard** day	He works **hard**.	**hardly** also exists - but the meaning is different. *He hardly works* is virtually the opposite of *he works hard*.
A **late** reply	He's working **late**.	**lately** also exists - but the meaning is different.
A **long** day	I **long** thought he'd never return.	**long**, adverb, has the meaning of *for a long time*.
The **Daily** Mirror	We check it **daily**.	
A **monthly** bill	I pay it **monthly**.	
The **wrong** answer	We went **wrong**.	**wrongly** also exists - but with a different meaning.
The **next** day	Who's going **next**?	

Short and long. The adverb phrases **for long** and **for short** are used with specific meanings, and **short**, following a quantity, means *"less than needed / expected"*.

> I won't be working in London **for long**. (= *for a long time*)
> He's called Archibald, but we call him Archie **for short**. (= *because it is shorter*).
> When we counted up the bottles, we found that we were seven **short**. (= *we had seven less than expected*).

3.1.2.3. Comparatives and superlatives:

Adjective and adverbial forms are also identical when adjectives are in a comparative or superlative form – unless this is formed with *more* or *most*:

> **Examples**: (adjective / adverb)
> better / **better**, fastest / **fastest**, more recent / **more recently**,
> There was a bright flash / The light was shining **brightly**
> I need a brighter light / The sun shone **brighter (more brightly)** in the evening.

3.1.3. Adverbs unrelated to adjectives

There are many common adverbs in English that are not related to adjectives; they can be found in all four types, as illustrated above. These adverbs include some important groups:

- Several common adverbs of frequency: **sometimes, seldom, often** etc.
- Several common adverbs of degree: **quite, very, too, enough**
- A number of "Sentence adverbs", which qualify whole clauses or sentences. (see § 3.1.4 below)

While these adverbs are themselves unrelated to adjectives, they often have synonyms that *are* formed from adjectives.

Examples

> Do you come here **often**?
>   (**Often** is a synonym of **frequently**)
> This is a **seldom**-performed opera by Wagner.
>   (**seldom** is a synonym of **rarely**)
> We **sometimes** go to the cinema on Fridays.
>   (**sometimes** is a synonym of **occasionally**)
> You are **quite** sure, aren't you?
> Your dissertation is **not** good **enough**.

Important: note that enough, as an adverb of degree, follows the adjective it is qualifying.

3.1.3.1. For the relative adverb **however**, see § 2.4.3.

3.1.4. Sentence adverbs

Adverbs qualifying a whole clause or a whole sentence

Some adverbs can apply (or in some cases only apply) to a whole sentence or statement. These can be:

- adverbs formed from adjectives, including modal adverbs, such as *consequently, possibly, clearly, inevitably, naturally, obviously, surprisingly, fortunately*, or
- other modal adverbs such as *maybe, even, just,* or
- **conjunctive adverbs** such as *therefore, perhaps, so, nevertheless, also...* For more on this see **Conjunctive adverbs.** (§ 3.4.)

To understand how **sentence adverbs** such as **therefore** or **perhaps** are adverbs like the others, just consider that **therefore** is a synonym of **consequently**, or that **perhaps** can be a synonym of **possibly**. Sentence adverbs are not conjunctions (like *but and for* or *as*), since conjunctions must come at the start of their clause; the position of sentence adverbs is not fixed, and they may be put at **different places** in the clause – though not in all cases.

Examples

> **Clearly** you have not understood what I am saying.
>
> You have **clearly** not understood what I am saying.
>
> **Maybe** you have not understood what I am saying.
>
> You have **maybe** not understood what I am saying.
>
> It's snowing, **therefore** (consequently) the match has been cancelled.
>
> It's snowing, the match has **therefore** (consequently) been cancelled.
>
> We will **obviously** try to find the right answer.
>
> **Naturally**, you will have to buy a ticket before you leave.
>
> You will have, **naturally**, to buy a ticket before you go in.

3.2. Prepositions

Definition
A preposition is a short word, for example **at, in** or **by**, that is most commonly used to show the relation between two nouns, two pronouns, or a noun and a pronoun. There are less than forty common prepositions in English.

Prepositions and prepositional adverbs

Many **prepositions** have related **adverbs**. This section looks at prepositions *and* at the adverbs that are related to prepositions, known as prepositional adverbs.

- **Prepositions** generally **precede the noun** they are referring to, but this is not always the case. They can – indeed sometimes they must – come at **the end of a sentence**, notably in some relative clauses with omission of who, or in some questions.
- **Prepositional adverbs** stand alone; there is no second noun or pronoun.
   Examples

Prepositions:
  The Queen is **at** home. Dinner is **on** the table. Go **to** bed.
Prepositional adverbs:
  They're standing **outside**. We're going **together**.

- For prepositions with verbs, see prepositional verbs (§ 1.18)

3.2.1. Prepositions of position and of direction

The table below lists the common English prepositions of position and of direction, and the related adverbs for each case. Many English prepositions can signify either direction or position; but this is not the case for all prepositions.

Prepositions of position and direction normally only introduce nouns or pronouns; a few, such as **into**, can occasionally introduce verb phrases. In this table, less common forms and rarely used equivalents are shown in brackets (--).

Denoting **position**		Denoting **direction**	
Adverbs	**Prepositions**	**Prepositions**	**Adverbs**
	across	across	
	at	at, to [1]	
* in, inside, (within)	in, inside, within	into	in, inwards
outside	outside	(out), out of [2]	out, outwards
(on)	on	on, onto	(on)
	(far from)	from	
overhead	over, above [3]	over (above)	(overhead)
underneath	under, (underneath)	under, (underneath)	
throughout	throughout	through	
below	below	below	
		up	upwards
		down	downwards
nearby	near (not far from)	(nearer)	
	beside (by)		
(alongside)	alongside	along	along
in between	between	(between)	
opposite	opposite		

Examples

Prepositions of position:
  Our friends live just **across** the street.
  I live **in** Windsor, **not far from** London.
  There are people **inside** the house.
  He lives **within** a mile of the airport, and right **by (beside)** the station.
  Our house is **opposite** the post office, just **off** the main road.
  There are problems **throughout** the programme.

Prepositions of movement:
  Take your boots **off** the table and put them **into** the box.
  Go **through** the town, **past** the church, then **over** the bridge.
  The child threw his plate **onto** the floor.
  The car went **up** the hill very slowly.

> **Adverbs of position:**
>   We're staying **in** tonight.
>   Look, the lights are **on**, there must be someone **inside**!
>   Our friends live **nearby**.
>   Take care! There's a drone **overhead**.
> **Adverbs of movement:**
>   I can't manage to put this nail **in**.
>   Look, now it's moving **inwards** and **downwards**.

Prepositions before a verb phrase:

He tricked me **into** paying far too much.

There are several other types of adverb, many of them derived from adjectives. ▶ For more on this, see Adverbs above (§ 3.1.)

Notes:

1. As prepositions of direction, "**at**" and "**to**" are <u>not</u> synonyms. "At" is not common as a preposition of direction, and is only used with the meaning of *towards* or *in the direction of*, and then only in some contexts. Compare these two sentences.
   I threw the ball to John.   I threw a cup at John.
   You can say *I'm going to London next week*,
   but it is impossible to say: "~~I'm going at London next week.~~"

2. In classic English, "**out of**" is the normal preposition of direction.
   Example: *I went **out of** the house.*
   But increasingly, particularly in spoken English, the **of** is being dropped, so you are likely to hear: *I went **out** the house*.

3. There is a small difference between "**over**" and "**above**" as prepositions of position. **Above** means *over, but not touching*.
   So you could say *There are clouds above London,*
   but it would be strange to say *There is fog above London.*

3.2.2. Prepositions of time

English has nine common prepositions of time: only one of these, **since**, can also be used as an adverb. In other cases, another word or phrase, sometimes quite similar, must be used.

Prepositions	Adverbs
before	beforehand, before that, earlier, previously
after	afterwards, then, later, subsequently
by	
in	
at	whereat, (thereat), whereupon
since	since
for	
during	meanwhile
until	

Examples: prepositions and adverbs of time

I'm playing football **before** lunch; but **earlier** I have an English lesson
He goes to Chicago **after** Detroit; **afterwards** he's going to Minneapolis.
The package must arrive **by** the end of the week / .... **by** Friday.
I'm leaving **in** five minutes. / I like going to England **in** the summer.
We're having lunch today **at** 12.30. / Everyone applauded **at** the end of the concert.
Online ticket sales began **at** 8 a.m, **whereupon** the whole programme crashed.
I've lived in London **since** the start of 1995 / .... **since** my childhood. [1]
She went to Australia 20 years ago, and we haven't seen her **since**.
I'm going to New York **for** a week in the summer
He worked in Dubai **for** three years. / ... **for** many years. [2]
During the holidays, he won the National Lottery. [3]
He's getting a new apartment tomorrow; **meanwhile** he's staying in a hotel.
My brother's staying in London **until** Friday.

Notes:

1. **Since** is used with moments in time, or with units of time, but not with numeric quantities. We cannot say: ~~since three weeks~~. **Since** can also be used as an adverb, with no following noun, and often strengthened with **ever**, as in:

He moved to Oxford in 1990, and he's been there ever since.

2. **For** is used with **numerals** (or undefined quantities).

3. **During** is used with **periods** of time; it is not used before numerals.

4. **Prepositions of time** cannot introduce verb phrases. When before, after, since and until are used in front of verb phrases, they are functioning as **conjunctions**, not as prepositions;

Before coming to London, he.... is the same as *Before he came to London, he…*

For more on For and since see the Linguapress online grammar

3.2.3. Other Prepositions - manner and other relations

English has eight common prepositions of manner, relation or agent:
against, among, by, for, of, with, without, except.
For full details about the use of **of**, see § 2.8 Possession, above.

Examples

> Manchester United are playing **against** Real Madrid next week.
> He was just one **among** many candidates.
> The Harry Potter books were written **by** J.K.Rowling.
> I've just bought a present **for** my mother.
> I'm going to Florida next week **with** my girlfriend.
> You can't play football **without** a ball.
> I told everyone **except** my brother.

3.2.3.1 *As used as a preposition*

Another word that may be used as a preposition is **as**, with the meaning of *in the condition of* or *in the role of,* or as in many common idioms on the model *as (adjective)… as (noun).*   For **as** as a conjunction, see § 3.3.2

Examples

> I'd like to think of you **as** a friend.
> That's really not too bad **as** a first attempt.
> **As** an adult, you ought to set a good example.
> It's **as** light **as** a feather.

3.2.3.2 *Prepositions introducing a verb phrase:*

> He broke his glasses **by** standing on them.
> You can't play football **without** using a ball.

Note that **by** and **without**, in the last two examples above, are effectively being used **prepositions** and not as **conjunctions**. So...

> While we **can** say
>   OK   Before *coming* to London... **or** Before *he came* to London....
> We **cannot** say
>   Not OK   He broke his glasses ~~by he stood~~ on them.

By is never used as a conjunction.

3.2.4. And a few more prepositions

Apart from these common prepositions, English has several more words or phrases that can be used as prepositions.

A few examples: **Apart from, following, amid, via, per.**

3.2.5. Ending a sentence with a preposition; is it OK?

Simple answer: **yes**! Lots of great writers have done so. Sometimes it may be better style to put the preposition in its normal place, before the noun, if this is possible; yet sometimes this is not possible or practical and a "*dangling preposition*", left on its own at the end of a sentence or clause, will be the best solution.

Look at these examples:

> 1. This is the talented young musician I was talking to you **about**.
> 2. What are you waiting **for**?

In these contexts – example 1 being a relative clause with omission of the relative pronoun, and example 2 a question requiring a preposition - it is perfectly good, indeed often **the best solution** possible in modern English, to leave the preposition at the end of the sentence.

The alternatives, without a *dangling preposition* are either rather formal (example1) or very archaic and formal (example 2), and should be avoided.

> 1. This is the talented young musician **about whom** I was talking to you.
> 2. **For what** are you waiting?

3.3. Conjunctions and connectors

> **Definition:**
> **Connectors** - also called **conjunctive words** - are words that link two similar elements in a sentence.

- The **four categories of connector**, which are explained below, are
    - **coordinating conjunctions**, such as **and** or **or**,
    - **subordinating conjunctions** such as **if, so that, because** or **while**. and
    - **correlating conjunctions** such as **neither... nor**
    - **conjunctive adverbs** such as **therefore** or **however**
- A small number of conjunctions and conjunctive adverbs can link individual words or phrases; but the majority can only link two clauses.
- A **coordinated clause or phrase must** follow the clause or phrase to which it is connected.
- A **subordinate clause normally** follows the main clause, but in some cases may precede it. See below.
- In most cases the difference between subordination and coordination is clear, but in some cases linguists disagree.
- A subordinate clause cannot stand alone: it needs a main clause to complete the sentence.

3.3.1. Conjunctions

3.3.1.1. Coordinating conjunctions

Coordinating conjunctions are used to link two clauses or phrases or words of equal value or equal status. There are only a small number of coordinating conjunctions in English: most sources repeat what others say, and list the following seven, using the convenient acronym FANBOYS.

- **for, and, nor, but, or, yet** and **so.**

This is a popular but misleading mnemonic. So forget fanboys, forget **for** and **so**, and go for the acronym **BANYO**.

- **For** can be forgotten, as it is hardly ever used as a coordinating conjunction in modern English. It has been replaced by **because** or **as**.... which are clearly subordinators.
- As for **so**, grammar books and websites provide contradictory and often ambiguous information. *So* let's clarify the situation.

When **so** implies **purpose** it is clearly a subordinating conjunction. The subordinate clause can come before or after the main clause.

> OK I bought a new camera **so** I could take better pictures.
>   OK **So** I could take better pictures, I bought a new camera.

When **so** implies **consequence** linguists disagree as to whether it is a coordinator a subordinator. But either way, the **so** clause must **follow** the main clause.

> OK I bought a new camera **so** I took better pictures.
>   NOT OK ~~So I took better pictures, I bought a new camera~~.

Many online dictionaries and grammar books do not distinguish coherently between the usage of **so** for purpose and **so** for consequence, or are very ambiguous on this point.

And and **or** can link individual words or clauses; **yet** and **but** normally only link clauses, but sometimes link two words. **Nor** cannot link words when it is a coordinating conjunction it can only do so in partnership with *neither*, as a correlative conjunction.

Usage:

Coordinating connectors give equal value to the two elements that they coordinate. They **must** be placed **between** the two elements that they coordinate.

Examples

> I want three beers **and** a glass of lemonade.
> He went to bed **and** went to sleep.
> You can have the chocolate mousse **or** the lemon tart
> They'll win, **or** they'll lose.
> This present is not for Peter, **but** for Paul.
> I bought a new dress that was not red **but** pink.
> We're going to Paris, **but** not to Rome.
> We're going to Paris, **but** we're also going to Rome.
> He was very tired **yet** very happy.
> The director was rather young, **yet** the company was successful.

3.3.1.1 Can you start a sentence with a conjunction?

A lot of grammar books claim that it is wrong to start a sentence with a conjunction. This is just **not true** ! And never has been.

Most of the great writers in the English language have used sentences starting with conjunctions. In the "King James" version of the Bible, which was the standard work of reference for style in the English language for three centuries, two of the first three sentences in the first chapter of the book of Genesis start with **And**.... These initial "ands" remain present in the main modern 20th or 21st century versions of the Bible, including the Contemporary English Version (CEV) and the American Standard Version (ASV).

In the beginning God created the heaven and the earth.
And *the earth was without form, and void;* ***and*** *darkness was upon the face of the deep.*
And *the Spirit of God moved upon the face of the waters.*

So yes, you **can** start a sentence with a conjunction.

3.3.2. Subordinating conjunctions

Subordinating conjunctions are used to link two clauses within a single sentence, when one clause is **subordinate to** the other. In other words, the subordinate clause clarifies, expands or explains the meaning of the main clause.

Some types of subordinate clause are introduced by **subordinating conjunctions**, others (such as relative clauses) are not. Common subordinating conjunctions include

- **as , because** and **since** (cause)
- **so** and **so that** (purpose)
- **although** and **though** (contrastive)
- **after, before, until, while,** etc. (temporal)
- **if, unless, as long as, provided, whenever, whatever** (conditional, indirect question)
- **that** (reported speech, indirect statement, consequential)

Usage

Subordinating conjunctions must come at the **start** of the **subordinate clause**.

There are two sorts of subordinate clauses.

1. **Most subordinate clauses** can come either **before or after** the main clause. So unlike coordinating conjunctions, subordinating conjunctions can stand at the start of a sentence.
2. But **indirect questions, relative clauses**, and subordinate clauses introduced by **that**, must normally be placed **after** the main clause, just like a coordinated clause *(Examples 12, 16 and 17)*.
3. **That** is very often **omitted**, specially in spoken English, at the start of a subordinated second main clause, as in examples 17 & 18.

3.3.2.1. Examples of subordinating conjunctions

In these examples, it is **not possible to invert** the two clauses in sentences **written in blue (12, 16 & 17).**

1. I'm going to London because I've got a new job.
2. Since it's raining, I'm going to the cinema this afternoon.
3. She didn't want any more wine, as she'd already drunk enough.
4. As she'd drunk enough, she didn't take any more wine.
5. I'm locking the door, so nobody can get in.
6. So he wouldn't forget to wake up, he set his alarm for 5.30.
7. Although I love him, I wouldn't want to marry him.
8. This book is good, though some bits of it are rather boring.
9. After I finished work, I went straight home.
10. Until they opened a new factory, they could not produce enough.
11. If you see anything suspicious, let me know at once.
12. He asked the policeman if he knew of a good restaurant.
13. Provided you can swim, you can come out on our yacht.
14. You can come out on our yacht, as long as you can swim.
15. I won't go there, whatever he says.
16. This ice-cream is so good, that I'm going to have another one.
17. The man said that he was born in New York.
18. I believe (that) he knows (that) we think (that) he's finished !

3.3.2.2. So as a subordinating conjunction

So is a **subordinating conjunction** when it is used to denote a **purpose**. A *so* clause denoting purpose does not usually come before the main clause, but it is not impossible *(example 6 above)*. When **so** is used to indicate **consequence**, i.e. with the meaning of *therefore* or *and similarly*, it is a **conjunctive adverb**.

3.3.3. Correlating coordinators

These can either correlate words, or phrases, or clauses (sentences). The main examples are:

> **both.... and, not only.... but also,** (combining correlators)
> **either...or , whether.... or not** (binary choice correlators)
> **neither.... nor,** (negative correlators)

Other correlating pairs include:

> **the more..... the more.....**
> **no sooner..... than...**
> **hardly ... than**

and a few other expressions. Note also that **many adjectives** can be used in their comparative form, preceded by **the**, as circumstantial correlating coordinators, as in.

> **The higher** they rise, **the harder** they fall.
> **The sooner** you stop doing that, **the better** (it will be).

Usage

When it is **words** or **phrases** that are coordinated, the coordinator normally has to precede the element it is correlating.

When **clauses** are correlated, the coordinators generally precede each correlated clause, but this is not always the case, as illustrated in examples 5 and 6 below.

Examples

> 1. This is **both** stupid **and** incomprehensible.
> 2. **Both** the president **and** the prime minister were there.
> 3. I can understand **both** his reasons **and** his arguments.
> 4. **Not only** can I hear him, **but also** I can see him
> 5. I can **not only** hear him, **but also** see him.
> 6. **Not only** can I hear him, I can see him (too).
> 7. I bought **not only** some blue suede shoes, **but also** a big cowboy hat.
> 8. It's **either** right **or** wrong.
> 9. **Either** it's right, **or** it's wrong
> 10. **Either** Mummy **or** Daddy will pick you up after school.
> 11. I'll go there **whether or not** I'm allowed to.

12. I'll go there **whether** I'm allowed to **or not**.
13. We're going home now, **whether** you like it **or not**.
14. **Neither** Paul **nor** Mary could come to my party.
15. I'm **neither** angry **nor** happy.
16. I **neither** like that man, **nor** dislike him
17. **I neither like that man; nor do I dislike him.**
18. I have **never** been to Florida on holiday; **nor** have I been there on business.
19. **The more** you earn, **the more** you spend.
20. **No sooner** had *I* opened the door, **than** the phone rang.
21. **Hardly** *had the plane* taken off, **than** the pilot reported some trouble.

Notes

- **Both ... and** can correlate words, and occasionally clauses (Examples 1 - 3)

- When **not only** <u>starts</u> a clause, the verb and subject of the first clause are inverted. (Example 4).

- **But also** can be omitted, after **not only** (Example 6).

- When **nor** introduces a clause, subject and auxiliary/modal verb are inverted. (Examples 16 - 18).

- **Neither** can be replaced by **not** or **never** in the first of two correlated clauses. (Example 18).

- When **no sooner** or **hardly** introduce clauses, auxiliary and subject are inverted. (Examples 20 & 21)

- For other uses of **whether**, see *Conditional clauses with whether* § 1.5.6. above.

3.4. Conjunctive adverbs

Conjunctive adverbs such as however *or* therefore

3.4.1. The nature of conjunctive adverbs:

> **Definition**:
> **Conjunctive adverbs** belong to the family of words known as *connectors*; they are a type of *sentence adverb* used in order to express a particular relationship between a first clause and a second clause that **follows**. In most cases, the two clauses will be separated by a semi-colon (;).

Conjunctive adverbs are very similar to **subordinating conjunctions**. The biggest difference is that conjunctive adverbs can frequently (but not always) be used in **a variety of positions** within the subordinate clause, whereas subordinating conjunctions **MUST** stand at the start of the subordinate clause.

Examples

> **Conjunctive adverb**: example **however** - *the position in the clause is flexible*
> * They bought a new car; it was **however** still too small for their family.
> * They bought a new car; it was still too small for their family, **however.**
> * They bought a new car; **however** it was still too small for their family.
>   They bought a new car; it was still too small **however** for their family.
>
> **Subordinating conjunction**; example **although** - *only one position is possible.*
> * **Although** they bought a new car, it was still too small for their family.

Conjunctive adverbs express different relationships between two clauses: for example

    Addition - also, besides, moreover,

    Consequence - consequently, hence, so, therefore, thus,

    Comparison – similarly, likewise,

    Contrast – alternatively, if not, however, nevertheless, otherwise,

    Confirmation - indeed, of course, naturally

Clarification - for example, for instance, namely, i.e.

In most cases, a conjunctive adverb will come **at the start** of the clause that it introduces; however this is not essential, and with many conjunctive adverbs **other positions** are possible.

More examples

> They played some music by the Beatles; **also / additionally** they did some songs by Elvis.
>
> They played some music by the Beatles; they **also / additionally** did some songs by Elvis.
>
> Let's buy that one, it's quite nice; **besides**, it's not expensive either.
>
> He's one of the directors; **consequently (hence, so)** he gets a BMW and a free parking space.
>
> He's one of the directors; he **consequently** (*but not* hence *nor* so) gets a BMW and a free parking space.
>
> You should have seen the doctor by now; **if not** you should make an appointment.
>
> You should have seen the doctor by now; you should make an appointment **if not**.
>
> Yes I loved that cocktail; **nevertheless** I won't have another one, thank you
>
> Yes I loved that cocktail; I won't have another one, **however**!
>
> The best students will all get prizes; **certainly** you'll be one of them.
>
> The best students will all get prizes; you'll **certainly** be one of them.
>
> You need to work less; **i.e.** you should take a holiday *(no other position is possible with* **i.e.**).
>
> You need to work less; you should take a holiday **for example** *(the position of* for example *may be flexible)*.

3.4.2. Usage

While they are both "connectors", It is important to distinguish between **conjunctive adverbs** and **subordinating conjunctions**, as they are not used in the same way. There are differences at two levels – the **position of the secondary clause** within the sentence, and the **position of the connector** within the secondary clause, as the next table shows.

Secondary clause.....	With a **conjunctive adverb**	With a **subordinating conjunction**
Examples	*Also, however, therefore, in fact, nevertheless, moreover,* *so* (meaning *therefore* or *and the same is true for*)	*Although, as, because, before, until, while, since,* *so** (in the sense of purpose), *so that*
Position of the **secondary clause** in the **sentence**	**Fixed: It must follow the main clause**	It can either precede or follow the main clause
Position of the **connector** (adverb or conjunction) within its **clause**.	Often **flexible**	**Fixed**: It must come at the **start** of the secondary clause

The case of too

Too means the same as **also**, but is used **after** the clause to which it applies *(examples 15 and 16 below)*. **Too** can also be used as an intensifier at the end of a secondary clause introduced by **and**.

Different meanings of so

So, as a conjunctive adverb, can either express
- a **consequence** (*see example 5*) or
- an **additional action** (*see example 6*).

When **so**, is used to introduce an additional action, it is necessary to invert the subject and the auxiliary. The same goes for the negative equivalent of **so**, which is **nor**. (*Examples 6 & 7 below*).

For **so** with the meaning of purpose, see so on Linguapress online grammar. Linguapress.com/grammar/.

Conjunctive adverbs in use.

More **Examples:**

1. I bought a new shirt; I **also** bought some new shoes.
2. I bought a new shirt; **also** I bought some new shoes.
3. I bought a new shirt; I bought some blue suede shoes **also.**
4. This is good cheese; **besides** it's made locally.
5. There's no more beer, **so** we'll have to drink lemonade.
6. I went to San Francisco last summer; **so** did my brother.
7. I didn't go to San Francisco, **nor** did my brother.
8. They won the state lottery, **therefore** they are now rather rich.
9. He found the solution; **thus** he was able to finish the project in time.
10. He found the solution; he was **thus** able to finish the project in time.
11. You can cross by ferry; **alternatively** you can take the Channel Tunnel.
12. They bought a new house; it was **however** still too small for their family.
13. They bought a new house; it was still too small for their family, **however**.
14. Stop making that noise, **otherwise** I'll call the police.
15. John went to London; Mary went there **too.**
16. I saw John and Mary **too.**

4 Sentences and clauses

4.1. Word order in statements

A colour-coded guide to English word-order

In the examples below, parts of the sentence are colour-coded: subjects in red, verbs in blue, direct objects in maroon, etc.

The man put the book on the table

Tomorrow they're going to London

Indeed he often gave the cat some milk

Linguapress.com

4.1.1. Subject, verb and predicate

▶ **4.1.1.1.** In a normal (declarative) sentence, the **subject** comes directly in front of the **verb**. The **direct object** (when there is one) comes directly after it:

Examples

> The man wrote a letter.
> People who live in glasshouses shouldn't throw stones.
> The president laughed.

▶ **4.1.1.2.** Note that by **the subject**, we mean not just a single word, but the subject noun or pronoun plus adjectives or descriptive phrases that go with it. The rest of the sentence - i.e. the part that is not the subject - is called **the predicate**.

Examples

> People who live in glasshouses shouldn't throw stones.
> I like playing football with my friends in the park.
> The child who had been sleeping all day woke up.

▶ 4.1.2. Other parts of the sentence

If a sentence has any other parts to it - indirect objects, adverbs or adverb phrases - these *usually* come in specific places:

4.1.2.1 The indirect object

The **indirect object** <u>follows</u> the **direct object** when it is formed with the preposition *to*:

The **indirect object** <u>comes in front of</u> the direct object if *to* is omitted.

Examples

> The doctor gave **some medicine to the child**.
> or: The doctor gave **the child some medicine**.

4.1.2.2. Adverbs or adverb phrases

Adverbs (single words) and **adverb phrases** (groups of words, usually formed starting with a preposition) can come in three possible places.

1) **Before the subject** (Notably with short common adverbs or adverb phrases, or sentence adverbs - *see below*).

Examples

> **Yesterday the man** wrote a letter.
> **At the end of March the weather** was rather cold.
> **Obviously the man** has written a letter.

2) **After the object** (virtually any adverb or adverb phrase can be placed here), **or**, with intransitive verbs, **after the verb.**

Examples

> The man wrote **a letter on his computer in the train**.
> The child **was sleeping on a chair in the kitchen**.

3) Or in **the middle of the verb group** (notably with short common adverbs of time or frequency).

> The man **has already written** his letter.
> The new version of the book **will completely replace** the old one.
> You **can sometimes get** real bargains in this shop.

4.1.2.3. Word order with "sentence adverbs"

Sentence adverbs (like *perhaps, surely, indeed, naturally, also* ....) relate to a whole clause or sentence, not just a single word. In most cases, they stand outside the clause they refer to, notably at the start of the clause. However, they may be placed elsewhere in the clause for reasons of stress or emphasis.

Examples

> Surely the man has already written his letter.
> Perhaps the man has already written his letter.
> The man has perhaps already written his letter
> ..., therefore the man had already written his letter.
> Naturally the man grew vegetables in his garden.
>   *Contrast this with:*
>   The man grew vegetables naturally in his garden.
>   *which has a quite different meaning.*

For more details, see § 3.1.4. Sentence adverbs.

4.1.2.4. Subject and verb, verb and object

In standard English, **nothing** usually comes between the subject and the verb, or between the verb and the object.

There are a few exceptions. The most important of these are *adverbs of frequency* and indirect objects without to. (Examples 1 and 2 below)

However, with adverbs of frequency, it is more normal to place them in the middle of the verb group (Example 3)

Examples

> The man *often* wrote his mother a letter.
> I *sometimes* have given my dog a bone.
> I have *sometimes* given my dog a bone.

The examples above are deliberately simple - but the rules can be applied even to complex sentences, with subordinate and coordinated clauses.

Example

> The director, [who *often* told his staff (to work harder),] *never* left the office before (he had checked his email.)

Exceptions

Of course, there are exceptions to many rules, and writers and speakers sometimes use different or unusual word order for special effects. But if we concentrate on the exceptions, we may forget the main principles, and the question of word order may start to seem very complex!

So here are just a few examples: you should realise that they exist, but **not** try to use them unless either they are essential in the context, or else you have fully mastered normal word order patterns. (Don't try to run before you can walk!)

A few examples of exceptional word order:

> **Never before had I seen** such a magnificent exhibition.
>   After *never* or *never before*, subject and verb **can** be - and usually are - inverted. Do not invert when *never* <u>follows</u> the subject!.
>
> **Hardly had I left** the house, than it started to rain.
>   When a sentence starts with *hardly*, subject and verb **must** be inverted.
>
> **Had I known**, I'd never have gone there.
>   Inversion occurs in unfulfilled hypothetical conditional structures when *if* is omitted. See § 1.5. on conditional clauses for more details.
>
> **The book that you gave me I'd** read already.
>   Emphasising a long object; in this example *The book that you gave me*, is placed at the start of the sentence for reasons of style: this unusual sentence structure is not necessary, just stylistic.

4.1.3. Complex or compound sentences.

Generally speaking, the order of words in the clauses of compound sentences follows the general principles of word order as explained above. For specific cases see

- § 1.5 Conditional clauses,
- § 3.3. Conjunctions and connectors,
- § 4.3. Reported questions,
- § 4.6. Relative clauses.

4.2. Word order in questions
How to form correctly ordered questions in English

Making correctly-formed questions in English is really **so simple**.... Almost all questions use the same structure. All you need to do is to remember this simple and common English phrase:

> How do you do?

The structure of almost every simple question in English is based on this same model:
   (**Question word if there is one**) - Auxiliary or modal - subject - main verb - (plus the rest of the sentence):

4.2.1. Question words - or wh- words

In English there are three types of question word
- **Interrogative pronouns** - who, whom, whose, what, which
- **Interrogative determiners** - which, what or whose (followed by a noun),
- **Interrogative adverbs** - where, why, how etc.

Examples

> Where did Jane Austen live?
> Whose is that car ?
> Did Arnold Schwarzenegger learn English quickly?
> How quickly did Arnold Schwarzenegger learn English?
> Has the bank sent us an invoice yet?
> How many books have you read this year?
> Is the new secretary being given her own laptop?
> Can the new secretary be given her own laptop?
> How quickly can the new secretary be given her own laptop?
> Is the new secretary nice?
> Why can't we have a second chance?

Important: take care!

In the interrogative, as in the negative, English verbs are **ALWAYS** made up of at least two elements, an auxiliary and the root verb.
In the interrogative there is only one exception to this rule, and that is certain tenses of the verb to be, as in example 2 above..
Examples:

> Are you ready?
> Is that true?
> Were they already at the pub when you got there?

For **all other verbs** - including **to have** - tenses that are formed with a single verb in an affirmative statement (i.e. the present simple and the simple past) are formed in the interrogative by the addition of the auxiliary **do**.

4.2.1.1. Modal verbs

Note that with **modal verbs** except *have to*, **do** is **not added** in order to form a question. The modal itself is the first verb unit. *Have to* is the only basic modal verb to which **do** needs to be used as the first verb in order to form a question.

Examples:

> Can you tell me the time, please?
> Should that child be crossing the road without an adult?
> Must you make such a noise?
> Do you have to make such a noise !?

4.2.2. Statements and questions with single-word tenses

> He had a good time. > Did he have a good time?
>   NOT Had he a good time?
> He lives in New York. > Does he live in New York?
>   NOT Lives he in New York?

4.2.3. Exceptions

Certain adverbs, notably short adverbs of frequency or time, can and indeed sometimes must be placed **between the auxiliary and the root verb**, as in statements. In questions, these adverbs are placed between the subject and the root verb.

> Has that French company yet sent us their order?
> Can the new secretary soon be given a bigger desk?
> **What sort of hats** do the ladies usually wear?

4.3. Reported questions

Reported questions and verb tenses in English

While expressing reported *statements* in English is relatively easy to master, putting direct *questions* into reported speech can often cause problems for the learner.

The simplest way to master the rules or structures is to start with a few varied direct questions, and use them as models. We will use the following Models:

> ► M1. Where is my jacket? (question using *to be*)
> ► M2. What is making that noise? (*Wh* word as subject,)
> ► M3 Does she like chocolate? (no question word present)
> ► M4. What are you doing? (*Wh* word as object).
> ► M5. Where do you live? (*Wh* word as adverb).

Preliminary points:

a) The main thing to remember is that in reported interrogatives, there is no inversion of subject and verb.

b) Reported speech can be introduced by a lot of different verbs, but most commonly by expressions such as "*He asked......, I wonder.....*" etc.

When there is no question word (as in model M3), indirect questions are introduced by *if* or *whether*. See below.

4.3.1. Reporting the present: simultaneous reporting.

This is not complicated. The verb tense in the reported question is the **same** as in the original question.

> **M1**. "Where is my jacket?" ▶ *He's asking where his jacket is.*
> **M2**. "What is making that noise?" ▶ *I wonder what's making that noise*
> **M3**. "Does she like chocolate?" ▶ *I wonder if (whether) she likes chocolate.*
> **M4**. "What are you doing?" ▶ *He's asking what you're doing.*
> **M4**. "What is he saying?" ▶ *I wonder what he's saying.*
> **M5** "Where does he come from?" *I wonder where he comes from.*

4.3.2. Reporting the past: deferred reporting

This is a little more complicated, but not impossible to master. It is the more common form of reporting. The verb in the reported question usually changes.

4.3.2.1. Reporting the past from the present.

If the reported question refers to a past situation, the verb in the reported question clause should go in the **past**. But if the reported question refers to a permanent or ongoing situation (**M11, M21,** etc.) , it *can* remain in the present.

> M1." Where is my jacket ?" ▶ *He asked where his jacket **was**.*
> M11 "Where is London ?" ▶ *He asked where London **is**.*
> M2. "What is making that noise ?" ▶ *I wondered what **was** making the noise.*
> M21 "Who lives in this house ?" ▶ *I wondered who **lives** in this house.*
> M3. "Do you want a chocolate?" ▶ *They asked (me) If I **wanted** a chocolate.*
> M31 "Do you speak English ?" ▶ *He asked (me) if I **speak** English.*
> M4. "What are you doing ?" ▶ *He asked what you **were** doing.*
> M41 "What are you doing ?" ▶ *He asked what you**'re** doing.*
> M4. "What is he saying?" ▶ *I asked what he **was** saying.*
> M5. "Where does he come from ?" ▶ *I asked him where he came from.*

In the examples above, the *jacket* (M1) has moved since the question was asked, but *London* (M11) has not moved. We can suppose that the *noise* (M2) has stopped, but that the person *still lives* (M21) in the house, and so on.

As for example M31, people often put the verb into the past tense in this type of reported question, though strictly this is not necessary, nor really correct. "*He asked me if I spoke English*" suggests that speaking English is something you can do one day, but not the next..

4.3.2.2. Reporting what was the *future* in the original question.

When a direct question using a **future** verb form is reported, the future form of the question clause becomes a conditional, or a future-in-the-past when what *was* the future is now the past.

   will > **would** − are going to > **were** going to − can > **could**, etc.

If the original future is **still** in the future (M11, M31, etc.), then the reported question remains in the future.

M1.	"Where will you be **tomorrow**?" ▶	*He asked **where I would be** **the following day**.*
M11	"Where will I be in 2040 ?" ▶	*I wondered where **I'll** be in 2040.*
M2.	"What will come next ?" ▶	*He asked what **would come next***
M3.	"Will you take me home?" ▶	*I asked if he**'d take** me home .*
M31	" Will he still be there in 2040 ?" ▶	*I wondered if he'll still be there in 2040.*
M4.	" What are you going to do ?" ▶	*He asked what I **was** going to do*
M41	"Who's she going to marry ?" ▶	*They asked who she's going to marry.*
M5.	"How will you survive?" ▶	*He asked me how I'd survive .*

4.3.3. Absolute and relative adverbs of time or place

English (like many other languages) has a series of adverbs of time and place which are *absolute* concepts, and strictly related to present time (the moment) or place. *Now, today, yesterday, tomorrow, in five minutes' time (etc.), here.*

In indirect questions or statements, the moment is not normally the same as it was when the question or statement was originally made. Therefore it is often necessary to change the adverb of time (or place) and use one that expresses a *relative* concept of time (or place). Here are the most common pairs:

- Today ▶ *that day, on the day….*
- Tomorrow ▶ *the next day, the following day*
- Yesterday ▶ *the day before, the previous day*
- Now ▶ *then, at that moment,*
- In five minutes' (etc.) time ▶ *five minutes (etc.) later*
- Here ▶ *there*

Example:

"Can you be here tomorrow?" would be reported as:
  *He asked if I could be **there** the following day.*

4.4. Tag questions

What are tag questions, and when are they used?

4.4.1. Definition and function

> **Tag questions** - also referred to as **question tags** - are very common, particularly in spoken English. They are short interrogative tags that can be added to the end of a declarative statement. Tags are usually added to a statement in order to express *opinion, possibility* or *probability*. Although they use an interrogative structure, tags are not real questions. They are **requests for confirmation...** or sometimes for contradiction.

4.4.2. Tag structures

4.4.2.1. Normal structure of tags

Question tags are normally formed on the model **verb > pronoun subject**. They are placed at the end of the sentence or clause. Using a standard interrogative inversion, they repeat the auxiliary used with the main verb and the pronoun corresponding to the subject of the main verb, as in these simple examples.

> That man is reading a good book, **isn't he**?
> Those students have passed their exams, **haven't they**?
> They didn't go to London last week, **did they**?

a). Standard tags

In standard tags, it is important to note that there is always an **opposition** between **affirmation** and **negation**. If the main verb is in the affirmative, the tag will be in the negative: conversely, if the main verb is in the negative, the tag will be in the affirmative.

> That lady is reading a good book, **isn't she**?
> Those students haven't passed their exams, **have they**?

b). "True-question" tags

Occasionally, but not often, speakers use "same-way tags", or "true-question" tags where there is **no opposition** between affirmation and negation. They are normally used in affirmative contexts: in this case both the main verb *and* the tag are in the affirmative. The speaker is either really asking for an answer, or else expressing doubt about the truth of the statement.

> **Examples**
> That lady **is** reading a good book, **is she**?
>   Meaning either: *Is that lady actually reading a good book?*
>   or: *I am really questioning whether that is a good book; I don't think so.*
> Those students **have** passed their exams, **have they**?
>   Meaning: *Have those students really passed their exams? That's surprising.*

It is important to remember that "same-way tags", or "true-question" tags are not common. It is useful to know that they exist, and what they mean; but students of English are best advised not to use them unless they are really sure that they understand the nuances or implications.

4.4.3. Use of tags

Tags are placed at the end of a statement or sentence; they are formed by repeating the auxiliary (**be, have, do** - **examples 1-6**) or the modal auxiliary (**can, must, might** etc. **examples 7 - 12**) used with the main verb, followed by a pronoun corresponding to the subject of the main verb. As stated above, there is normally an **affirmative/negative contrast** between the main verb and the tag.

Examples

> 1. The Queen's over 90, **isn't she**?
> 2. Those new shoes weren't very expensive, **were they**?
> 3. You've remembered all the instructions, **haven't you**?
> 4. The kids hadn't had anything to eat, **had they**?
> 5. You did remember to turn off the gas, **didn't you**?
> 6. The secretary didn't like the new boss, **did she**?
> 7. He can sing quite well, **can't he**?
> 8. You can't come to the concert tonight, **can you**?
> 9. We shouldn't continue without the guide, **should we**?
> 10. You really ought to get permission first, **oughtn't you**?
> 11. You couldn't understand anything he said, **could you**?
> 12. The students really have to work hard, **don't they**? *

Note the last example above: tags following the **modal auxiliary** "*have to*" (as opposed to the **past auxiliary** *have*) are forms of the auxiliary *do*, not *have*, even if the main verb is in the affirmative.

If the main verb does not use an auxiliary (i.e. it is in the simple present or simple past tense), the tag will be formed using a form of the auxiliary *do*, just like the interrogative and negative forms of these tenses.

Examples

> The Queen lives in Buckingham Palace, **doesn't she**?
> Those new shoes look very expensive, **don't they**?
> You remembered all the instructions, **didn't you**?
> This one looks rather interesting, **doesn't it.**
> People who eat too much **get** fat, **don't they**?

Note the last example above: the tag reflects the **main verb** of the sentence of course; *get* not *eat*.

If the main verb is accompanied by several auxiliaries, including modal auxiliaries, the tag reflects back to the **first** of the auxiliaries used.

Examples

> The Queen **might** have been in Buckingham Palace**, mightn't she**?
> You **should** have been paying more attention**, shouldn't you**?
> They **could** have lost all their money in Las Vegas**, couldn't they**?
> He ought to have been able to answer all the questions**, oughtn't he**?
> He might have had to buy a new computer**, mightn't he**?
> They can't have had to stop already**, can they**?

Used with reported speech and similar structures, it is important to remember that the tag reflects the **main verb** of the sentence, not the verb of the reported speech.

Examples

> He **said** you were very clever, **didn't he**?
> It **looks** like we ought to be getting out of here quickly, **doesn't it?**
> They **didn't think** it was particularly easy, **did they**?
> The judge **believes** that the accused is innocent, **doesn't he**?
> You **were telling** us about what you did in New York, **weren't you**?
> You **don't think** there's anything wrong with my idea, **do you**?

4.4.4. Alternative form of negative tags

Just occasionally people express negative tags without contracting the word **NOT** to **n't**.
IMPORTANT! In uncontracted tags, the word order is different, as **NOT** follows the verb: Compare the following:

> This point has already been clearly explained, **has it not**?
> It's good, isn't it / It's good, **is it not**?
> They're very late, aren't they / They're very late, **are they not**?
> You've seen the show, haven't you /
> You've seen the show, **have you not**?

Uncontracted tags are used particularly in written English, where the contracted form might seem too informal. They are also used in some dialects, or by speakers wishing to sound more formal.

4.5. Negative structures

Different ways of expressing negation in English

> **Different ways of expressing negation**
> When Mick Jagger famously sang   **I can't get no satisfaction....**
> he was not helping students of English. Jagger was using what we call a "double negative": and the logical result of a double negative is really an affirmative statement. As all mathematicians know , **-1 x -1 = +1.**
> **Double negatives** are quite common in slang and in spoken English; but they are not acceptable in written English. The expression *I can't get no satisfaction* – which thus technically means *I can get satisfaction* – is however a useful example, as it shows that there is more than one way of transforming an affirmative statement into a negative statement. In fact there are several ways.
> **Negation can be expressed by:**
>   1) Adding a negative particle to the verb, or
>   2) Adding negation to a noun or pronoun, or
>   3) Using a negative adverbial phrase, or
>   4) Using neither and nor when there are two expressions to be negated, or
>   5) Adding a negative prefix or suffix to an adjective.
> *But doing two of these at the same time will produce a double negative, so theoretically an affirmation, as in the example.*

4.5.1. Negative forms of the verb

In most cases a negative meaning is given to a **verb** by adding the negative verbal particle **NOT**. In some cases, **not** is replaced by **never**.

 Not (sometimes shortened to **n't**) normally follows the principal auxiliary or modal verb in a verbal structure. In the few cases where there is no auxiliary or modal (present simple or past simple affirmative tenses), it follows a reconstituted auxiliary, *do* or *did*. The choice between **not** and **n't** is a matter of style. **Not** is generally preferred in written English, **n't** in spoken English

Examples

> He lives in London / He **does not** live in London
> I can see you   / I **cannot** see you / I can't see you
> I like those photos / I **don't like** any of those photos
> The man lost all his money / The man **did not** lose all his money
> I should eat (some) more chocolate / I **shouldn't** eat (any) more chocolate.
> You ought to have gone home / You **ought not to** have gone home.
> I may be able to finish in time / I **may not** be able to finish in time.

Never is used in the same way as **not**, except when the verb is in the simple present or simple past tense. With **never**, there is no need to add a missing auxiliary using a form of do.

Examples

> He plays tennis / He **never** plays tennis. (*but not* He does never play)
> I saw the Queen yesterday / I **never** saw the Queen yesterday.
> I've been to London . / I've **never** been to London.
> You should eat a lot of chocolate / You should **never** eat a lot of chocolate.
> You ought to have done that / You ought **never** to have done that.
> I may be able to finish this. / I may **never** be able to finish this.

See also pages on *to have* (§ 1.12) for **important distinctions** between the different forms of the negative with to **have** as a **main verb** or as an **auxiliary**. (Specifically, when to use **haven't** and when to use **don't have**, for example).

4.5.2. Negating a quantifier

The particle **not** can also be added to the quantifiers **much** or **many**, to form the small-quantity quantifiers **not much** or **not many**. It can also be added to **enough**, to give the meaning of *insufficient quantity.*

Examples

> **Not many** people came to the concert last night.
> It's still pretty poor, and **not much** better than it used to be.
> **Not enough** people bought tickets, so the show was cancelled.

4.5.3. Negation using a noun or pronoun

Less frequently, a negative meaning may be implied by attaching a **negative particle** to a **noun** group, either the subject or the direct object of a sentence. In this case, the negative particle that is used is **no**. **No** is sometimes combined with *-one, -thing, -where,* etc. to make negative indefinite pronouns, **no one, nobody, nothing, nowhere**, etc.

Examples

Trees grow on the moon / **No** trees grow on the moon.
I can see someone / I **cannot** see anyone / I can see **no one.**
The man lost time / The man lost **no** time
I should eat more chocolate / I should eat **no** more chocolate.
There's something in that box / There's **nothing** in that box.
The riders were able to finish the race/ **No** riders were able to finish the race.

None of is used in the same way as **no**, except that it is followed by a definite article, another determiner, or a pronoun. When only two people / items are concerned, none is normally replaced by **neither**.

Examples

The riders were able to finish the race **/ None of** the riders were able to finish the race.
Your shoes are clean / **None of** your shoes are clean.
I like those photos / I like **none of** those photos.
Did you eat some chocolates? / Did you eat **none of** the chocolates?
In the event, **none of** us were right, all three of us were wrong.
In the event, **neither of** us were right, we were both wrong.

For more on negation with nouns, see § 2.6. Some and Any as quantifiers.

4.5.4. Negation using an adverb phrase

It is also possible to add a negative meaning to a **sentence**, by including an **adverb phrase with a negative meaning**. The most common group of negative adverbial phrases are formed using the word **without**, or a preposition followed by **no**.

Examples

> You can have some whisky / You can **do without** whisky.
> He's walking with a stick / He's walking **without a stick**.
> He did it for a good reason / He did it for **no** reason at all.
> I want you to do it with me / I want you to do it **without** me.

4.5.5. Neither and nor - linking two negative statements

Neither and **nor** are used to link a pair of negative pronouncements. **Nor** can be used by itself to introduce the second of a pair of negative statements, even if a normal **not** structure is used in the first one. **Neither** and **nor** can be attached to verbs, or to nouns (subjects or objects), or even to prepositional phrases.

When **nor** introduces a **second main clause**, the subject and the auxiliary or modal are **inverted**. See examples 3 to 5 below.

Examples

1. He **neither** looks like a gentleman, **nor** talks like a gentleman.
2. I can **neither** see it **nor** hear it.
3. I didn't agree with what he said. **Nor did I** believe him.
4. He hasn't eaten for three days; **nor has he** slept.
5. They can't find the problem; **nor can they** explain why it happened.
6. I like **neither** your appearance **nor** your attitude.
7. **Neither** the President **nor** the Prime minister was (were) present.
8. I could convince him **neither** with my arguments **nor** with my warnings.
9. You should wash this in water, but **neither** with soap **nor** with detergent.

4.5.6. Negation using negative adjectives

An affirmative statement can be turned into a negative statement by adding a **negative prefix or suffix** to an appropriate adjective.

Examples

> This is possible > This is **im**possible.
>
> You are being very cooperative > You are being very **un**cooperative.
>
> The border guards were friendly > The border guards were **un**friendly.
>
> I'm very pleased with my results > I'm very **dis**pleased with my results.
>
> He's being very sensible > He's being very sense**less.**

4.5.7. Negation with tag questions

Negative **tags** attached to the end of affirmative statements have the structure and appearance of negative questions, but they do not really express a negative value, and they are not really questions; they are essentially an expression of minor doubt, or a means of requesting confirmation of a statement or an opinion.

▶ For more on this, see Tag questions (§ 4.4.) above.

4.6. Relative clauses

Forms and functions of relative clauses in English grammar

> This page looks at standard **relative clauses**, using the principal relative pronouns *who that* and *which*.
>
> For information on *nominal relative clauses*, and on other relative pronouns or adjectives such as *whatever* or *when* or *whenever*, ▶ see Relative pronouns (§ 2.4.2.)

Relative clauses can cause trouble in English, specially when they begin with less common forms of the pronoun *who*, such as **"whom"** or **"whose"**. And there's another problem: when to use **which** and when to use **that**? This topic is dealt with in nine parts.

    4.6.1. Clauses with the relative pronoun as subject

    4.6.2. Clauses with the relative pronoun as object and the question of whom

    4.6.3. The relative pronoun as a possessive

    4.6.4. Relative clauses starting with a preposition

    4.6.5. More complex structures

    4.6.6. Defining and non-defining relatives, and punctuation.

    4.6.7. Using that

    4.6.8. Relative clauses which qualify a whole sentence, not just a noun.

    4.6.9. Omission of the relative pronoun.

4.6.1. Clauses with the relative pronoun as subject

1.1. When the relative pronoun is **subject** of a clause and refers to a **human**, the relative pronoun *who* is generally used.

Examples

> The man **who** lives next door is 99.
> I know someone **who** eats red hot chilli peppers.

Sometimes, **who** is replaced by **that**, especially in American English and in spoken language:

Examples

> The boy **that** lost his watch was careless.
>   *However,*

> The boy **who** lost his watch was careless.   *is also quite possible.*
> *After the antecedent **those**,* who *or* that *can be used*
> Those **who** can swim should go first.
> Those **that** can swim should go first.

1.2. If the relative is the **subject** of a clause and refers to an **inanimate** antecedent, *which* or *that* must be used.

Examples

> The book **that**'s on the table is mine.
> The book **which** is on the table is mine.

1.3. IMPORTANT

Omission: As **subject** of a clause, the relative pronoun **can never be omitted.** However, the relative clause can be completely omitted.

> **Examples**
> ~~The book **is** on the table is mine~~ is quite impossible, but
>   The book on the table is mine   is perfectly acceptable.

4.6.2. Clauses with the relative pronoun as object

Even if the relative pronoun is the object of the clause, it still stands **at the start** of the clause.

4.6.2.1. When the relative pronoun is the **direct object** of the clause, and refers to a **human**, the pronoun used is either *whom* or *that*.

Examples

> The man *whom* I saw yesterday is 99.
>   The man *that* I saw yesterday is 99.

Omission: when it is the object of the relative clause, the relative pronoun can often be omitted, in both spoken and written styles.

>   The *man I saw* yesterday is 99.

The relative, whether mentioned or not, is the **only** object of the clause, and there can be no second object following the verb.

Thus we **cannot say or write:**

> ~~The man whom I saw him yesterday is 99~~.
>   nor ~~The man I saw him yesterday is 99.~~

The question of whom

Whom is not used very often: *that*, or omission of the relative pronoun, are much more common. In spoken English, *whom* is going out of use as an object pronoun, replaced by *that* or omitted entirely. In direct questions, it is usually replaced by *who* in spoken English except in very formal style.

Examples

> **Whom** did meet last night ? *sounds very formal.*
>   *Most speakers would ask:* **Who** did you meet last night?

4.6.2.2. When the relative pronoun is the **direct object** of the clause, and refers to **an *inanimate object*** , the pronoun used is *which* or *that*.

> The book *that* I was reading was very interesting,
>   *or* The book *which* I was reading was very interesting,
>   *or* The **book I was reading** was very interesting.

4.6.3. The relative pronoun as a possessive

Whose is required with both animate and inanimate antecedents: it is the only derivative of *who* which can refer to animates *and* inanimates.

Examples

> I know someone **whose** sister is a nurse.
>   The man **whose** car I borrowed is very rich.
>   I chose the set **whose** price was reduced.

4.6.4. Relative clauses starting with a preposition

Note how to form relative clauses after prepositions: we use **preposition + which** for inanimates or things, **preposition + whom** for people. Stylistically, this is quite formal.

When referring to places or locations (but **not** to objects), **in which** is often replaced by **where**; when referring to a moment in time **in which / at which** is sometimes replaced by **when.** (See also § 2.4.2.4 above).

Examples

> The man **with whom** I was talking was angry.
>   The chair **on which** he sat down collapsed.
> In the town **where / in which** I was born …
> The car **in which** / ~~where~~ I was sitting …
> Describe the moment **at which / when** you first became suspicious

4.6.5. More complex structures
Examples

> **1. Preposition + possession:**
> The player **on whose** skills the match most depended, was the goalkeeper.
> It is to my parents, **thanks to whose** generosity I was able to complete my studies, that I am most grateful.
>
> **2. Selective possession:**
> The café, **most of whose** customers had deserted it, had to close.
> The writer, **the first of whose** books had been a bestseller, was a coal miner.
> There are several ways to go from London to Scotland, **the fastest of which** is of course by plane.

4.6.6. Defining and non-defining relative clauses

A **defining** relative clause (also called a **restrictive** or **integrated** relative clause) is one which is essential for the understanding of a statement. In this case **commas are not required** before and after the relative clause.

Examples

> **Protesters who** smash windows will be arrested.
> **Cars which** can do 150 miles per hour are pointless.
> **Cars that** can do 150 miles per hour are pointless.

The first example tells us that "protesters **who smash windows**" will be arrested; but suggests that those who do **not** smash windows will **not** be arrested. The word "protesters" in this example is restricted by the relative clause that defines it.

In a **non-defining** relative clause (also called a **non-restrictive** relative clause or a **supplementary** relative clause), the relative clause is **not** essential for an understanding of the sentence. In cases like this, **commas are** usually required before and after the relative clause.

Examples

> **Protesters, who** are mostly aged under 30, want to express an opinion.
> **Cars, that** were invented at the end of the 19th century, have become a vital part of modern life.

In the first of these examples, the question of age is not an essential bit of information. In the second, it is obvious that it is *cars in general*, not cars from the late 19th century, that are a vital part of modern life. The relative clause can be omitted without making the sentence meaningless. Compare these two examples:

Examples

1. **People who eat** too much tend to have poorer health.
2. **Sportsmen, who watch** their diet, are not usually over-weight.

4.6.6.1. *One of* + *a relative clause*

When **one of + group noun** is followed by a relative clause, the **verb** in the relative clause will be in the singular if the relative clause – with or without commas - is non-defining (just applies to **one)**, in the plural if it defines **the group.** Take care; some grammar books give wrong information on this point, but choosing either a singular verb or a plural verb is the only way, in this case, of avoiding ambiguity.

Examples

1. Just **one** of my friends **who was born** in Scotland wears a kilt.
2. Just **one** of **my friends who were born** in Scotland wears a kilt.

In example 1, only one of these friends was born in Scotland; in example 2 the speaker has several friends who were born in Scotland.

4.6.7. Using that instead of who or which in relative clauses

- The relative pronoun **that** may be used in English, particularly American English, in defining relative clauses.
- That **cannot replace** who in **non-defining** relative clauses.

Examples

Protesters, who (that…no !) are mostly aged under 30, want to express an opinion.

However use of **that** instead of **who** or **which** in **defining clauses** is an **option**, not a rule, and a source of plenty of confusion.

Some grammar books suggest that **which** or **who** *must* be used in defining relative clauses, and that **that** *must* be used in non-defining relative clauses. This is not correct, neither in British nor American English, and countless quotes from the best authors demonstrate this.

Don't rely on grammar checkers that come with word-processing software.

Experience shows that they are not terribly good at distinguishing **defining** from **non-defining** relative clauses, and may want to wrongly "correct" a user's punctuation.

4.6.8. Relative clauses which qualify a whole sentence

Sometimes we use a relative clause to qualify not just a noun or pronoun, but a whole sentence or clause. In such cases, the relative clause is introduced by **which**, never by ~~that or what~~.

Examples

> He drank too much, **which** is why he was sick.
> It was raining yesterday, **which** was a pity.
> There aren't enough tables in the exam room, **which** is rather a problem.

4.6.9. Omission of the relative pronoun

See sections ▶ 4.6.1, 4.6.2, and 4.6.4 above.

When the relative pronoun is omitted in a prepositional relative clause (as seen in § 4.6.4)., the **preposition must** come at the end of the clause. This is true even if the end of the clause is also the end of the sentence. This is not a problem. As stated above, omission of the relative pronoun in prepositional relative clauses is **normal style** in modern English. It is sometimes suggested that ending a sentence with a "dangling preposition" is bad style and should be avoided; but in this case, leaving the preposition to the end of the sentence is not just acceptable, it may be essential.

Examples

> I hope that this is a page you'll really learn something **from**.
> Our company currently has enough financial reserves to get **by with**.
> The project our team is currently working **on** is of huge potential significance.

4.7. Punctuation

Punctuation is an **essential** (not optional) aspect of written communication in all European languages. Most languages use the same signs and conventions; and while these are used in the same general manner in all languages, they are not used in exactly the same way in all languages. Without punctuation, most texts in written English would be impossible or very hard to understand.

In English there is a certain flexibility over punctuation; and British and American conventions are not identical. Nevertheless there are some clear rules that **must** be followed, either because they are the accepted norm, or because they help to avoid ambiguity or just make a sentence comprehensible. One classic example shows this conclusively! *"Let's eat, Grandma!"* does not mean the same as *"Let's eat Grandma."* The main rules and conventions are listed below.

Punctuation in written language corresponds to **pauses** and **intonation** in spoken language.

4.7.1. Different types of punctuation

Punctuation is mostly made up of **signs**, but is also marked by **spaces**, **line-breaks** and the **capitalisation** of some words.

A list of the main punctuation elements in English

- . The **full stop** (British English) or **period** (American English)
- : The **colon**
- ; The **semi-colon**
- , The **comma**
- ? The **question mark**
- ! The **exclamation mark**
- ' The **apostrophe**
- — The **dash**
- - The **hyphen**
- " "   **Inverted commas**, or **quotation marks**
- ( )   **Brackets**, or **parentheses**
  plus Use of **paragraphs** and **capital letters**

4.7.2. Use of paragraphs

IMPORTANT: The use of paragraphs is one of the most widely ignored rules of good writing, notably by students writing dissertations or essays, or managers writing reports or letters .

Paragraphs divide a long block or text into **manageable units**. There is no hard and fast rule about when to start a new paragraph; but there are some conventions to follow.

Good paragraph practice

Avoid having more than five sentences in a **single paragraph.** Three-sentence paragraphs are just fine.

Start a **new paragraph** when you move to a new idea or a new topic.

A paragraph can contain just a **single** sentence. This is often the case in journalistic style, when writers are trying to express ideas simply and bluntly.

4.7.3. The full stop or period

- The full stop (GB) or period (USA) is used to separate sentences. In this case, it must be followed by a capital letter.
- It is also traditionally used at the end of shortened titles, such as **Capt.** , **Prof. Lt.** (Lieutenant), **Cllr.** (Councillor) etc. ; but it is often omitted in British English with **Mr** (or Mr.) (never write *Mister* in full) or **Mrs** (or Mrs.)., and never used after **Miss**.
- It is used at the end of common abbreviations, such as Mon. (for *Monday*) or etc. (for *etcetera*).
- It is not required, though occasionally used, for writing acronyms or initials, such as NATO, UNESCO, the UK, the FBI,

Examples

Peter arrived in Singapore in January 1996, on his twenty-second birthday. Less than a year later, he had married the boss's daughter Yi Ling.

I'd like you to meet Mr Mark Porter, Miss Elizabeth Taylor, Capt. Eliot Saunders and his wife Mrs Saunders.

I began teaching at UCLA on Mon. 29th Aug. 2018, after five years with UNICEF.

4.7.4. The colon

Colons are used to **separate** (a) **two main clauses**, or (b) **a main clause and a phrase**, when the second clause or phrase provides an **example** or an **illustration** of what is said in the first clause.

Examples

> I told him what he ought to **do: he** should tell her at once that he'd lost his job.
> I only like three sorts of **fruit: apples,** pears and bananas.

4.7.5. The semi-colon

- Semi-colons are used to **separate two long main clauses**, when they both have the same subject, and/or are both part of a single topic or idea; they are particularly used when the second clause starts with a conjunction.
- Semi-colons are also used as a kind of "**super comma**", in sentences which have a number of commas, and where one or two breaks need more emphasis than others.

Examples

> I had seen lions and rhinoceros in the zoo, most recently at Whipsnade zoo, which is near **London; but** I'd never before seen them in the wild in their natural environment.
> The students, who'd been there for three days, were sleeping in **tents; as for** the medical staff, they had a bungalow to sleep in.
> I'd been to England, Scotland, and Wales, which I particularly **enjoyed; and** also to France, Spain, and Portugal.

4.7.6. The comma

Commas are principally used to separate clauses, to put words into relief in a sentence, or to separate elements in a list.

Often the use of commas can be a matter of personal taste or style; however some commas are essential:

1. Commas are **required** with **non-defining relative clauses** (but **not** with defining relative clauses) (See § 4.6.6. above) .
2. Commas (or semi-colons) are **needed** to separate **contrasting parts** of a sentence, including two short main clauses.

3. Commas are **recommended** in all but very short **lists**; sometimes they are **essential**, as in example 3b below, which is **incomprehensible** without them.
4. Commas are **required** at the end of **quoted direct speech**, when this is followed by words like *he said, they told us* or *said the President.*

Examples

1a. Elton Jo**hn, wh**o is a great pian**ist, is** a campaigner for gay rights.
1b. Scotch Whis**ky, wh**ich has to be impor**ted, is** popular in Brazil.
2. Peter was just getting out of b**ed, bu**t his wife Myriam was already washed dressed and in the car.
3a. Would you please bring me three appl**es, tw**o banan**as, a pe**a**r, and** a carrot.
3b. You can choose different colour-schem**es, in**cluding black and whi**te, p**ink and pur**ple, br**ight oran**ge, and** yellow and green.
4a. "I'm a hundred and one years ol**d," the** old man said.
4b. "I don't know what you are talking abo**ut," an**swered Jennifer.

4.7.7. The apostrophe

Apostrophes are required in **two**, and only two, different situations.

- **Possession: before a final s** added to a singular noun, or **after the s** of a plural noun.

- **Omission**: To indicate that a letter or more than one letter has been **omitted**.

An apostrophe **is NEVER required** before an **s marking a plural.**
An apostrophe **is not required** in the **possessive adjective** its, only for **it's** when this is a contraction of **it is.**

Examples

This is my **brother's** bicycle.
The manager was very disappointed with the **players'** poor performance.
Do**n't** go away, **it's** hard enough with just two of us.

181

4.7.8. Capital letters

Capital letters are required in a number of different situations:

1. All **proper nouns** (names), and **adjectives formed from proper nouns**, must be capitalized, unless the semantic connection between the adjective and the noun has been lost (as in french fries, which are not usually French).
2. Capitals must also be used for **titles**, whether we are talking about human titles (such as *General, Prince*, etc.), or the titles of books, films etc. In titles, capitals tend to be used on lexical words (nouns, verbs) but not on functional words (such as *Gone with the Wind*).
3. Capitals must be used when writing **days of the week, months of the year**, but not for the names of the seasons.
4. Capitals must be used throughout **initials** or **acronyms**
5. And finally, of course, every **new sentence** must start with a capital letter.

Examples

My Dutch friend from Amsterdam speaks good English, and he loves Italian pasta and German beer; but he never eats potatoes, not even french fries.

General Eisenhower became President of the United States; one of his favourite books was "A Connecticut Yankee in King Arthur's Court".

The campsite is open in the summer months of July and August, and in autumn until the last Sunday in October.

The United Nations has several subsidiary organisations, including UNICEF and UNESCO.

Each new sentence must start with a capital. There are no exceptions to this rule.

4.7.9. Other marks of punctuation

Quotation marks

Quotation marks are required at the start and at the finish of all direct speech, even after a short interruption by a dialogue tag like *he said*.

Question marks

Question marks are required at the end of all direct questions, but are **not** necessary, and often considered wrong, at the end of indirect questions.

Exclamation marks

Exclamation marks can replace full stops at the end of a sentence, to express surprise. Do not over-use them, as this is bad style.

Other punctuation marks

Long dashes can be used, rather like **brackets**, to put part of a sentence into parentheses, specially if alternative forms of punctuation could lead to ambiguity.

Hyphens are used to form common compound nouns or adjectives, or else to clarify the relationship between words in a noun group. While some common compound words are always hyphenated, in many cases it will be a matter of personal choice, and dictionaries do not always agree.

For detailed rules on the use of hyphens in English, see Rossiter: Problem words in English, section 24.

Examples

> "I was in the garden," he said, "but I didn't see anything."
> "Are you sure?" asked the policeman.
> The policeman asked if he was sure.
> "Help! "
> Nothing quite so exciting has ever been done before!
> There are three large strange animals – no-one knows exactly what they are – that are sometimes seen on the moor at night.
> It was a heart-breaking story about a used-car salesman and his daughter-in-law.

4.8. Language and style

Written and oral styles of English

In any language, different styles of expression are appropriate in different situations. We can go from the formal to the informal, the written to the spoken, from technical language (or jargon) to slang.

There are no "rules" as such; nevertheless, there are plenty of features which distinguish **formal** styles from **informal** styles. Here are some of them.

4.8.1. Basic principles of English style

Note: these are **principles or conventions**: *they are* **by no means** *to be considered as "rules".*

a) The more **formal** a document is, the more it will use inanimate nouns (i.e. things, processes, ideas, rather than people) as the subjects of sentences.

b) The more **formal** language is, the more it is likely to use **passive** structures (see § 1.8. above: Passives.)

c) The more **formal** language is, the more **verbal nouns** (i.e. nouns like *development* or *creation*) it will use.

d) The more **formal** a document is, the more words of **Latin** origin it will use.

Conversely

a) The more **informal** or spontaneous language is, the more it will use **humans** as the subjects of sentences.

b) The more **informal** a text is, the **less** it will use passive structures,

c) The more **informal** a text is, the more it will use **verb** structures where a choice is possible (i.e. *develop* or *create*) instead of verbal nouns.

b) The more **informal** or spoken a text is, the more words of **Germanic** origin it will use.

From formal to informal, written to spoken English

Here are some **examples**; in each case, **the same idea** is expressed using three different levels of formality: look at the different changes that occur, as we move from a **formal style** via an **intermediate style** and to an **informal one.**

> **1.** The inclement climatic conditions obliged the President to return earlier than scheduled.
> The president was obliged to return earlier than planned due to poor weather conditions.
> The president had to go back sooner than planned because the weather was so bad.
> **2.** Please await instructions before dispatching items.
> Please wait for instructions before sending items off.
> Don't send anything off until you're told to.
> **3.** Essential measures should be undertaken at the earliest opportunity.
> One should undertake any necessary measures at the earliest opportunity.
> You should do whatever you have to as soon as you can.
> **4.** Prior to the discovery of America, potatoes were not consumed in Europe.
> Before America was discovered, potatoes were not eaten in Europe.
> Before they discovered America, Europeans didn't eat potatoes.

Written and spoken versions of a language use different styles, different registers. To talk in "written English" may be no more appropriate than to write using a "spoken" variety of English. Generally speaking, written English is always more formal than spoken English. Nevertheless, there are informal forms of written English (notably in fiction and in the popular press), and formal styles of spoken English, in particular "discourse", or prepared speech.

Written style can also be affected by the **length** of sentences used, the length of paragraphs, and other features of punctuation.

The same idea expressed in six different styles:

In the following examples, the same message is expressed in **six** different styles, from an extremely formal written style, to a very informal spoken style. Note in particular how the **colour coded word groups** evolve.

In order to demonstrate a full range of styles using a single "message", it is necessary to choose a subject or topic which people actually write or talk about in a whole range of contexts. These examples show the different styles, from the very formal to the informal, that could be used for expressing a message about government fiscal policy (or, to put it less formally, government tax policy). Different parts of the message are colour-coded: see how they change from one style to the next. Note that the British currency is formally known as "**Sterling**", and most often spoken about as "**the Pound**".

a) Jargon, very formal.
*This is the style of language used in official reports, technical studies, etc. It is exclusively a style of written English, full of **verbal nouns, technical** words and **passives**.*

♦ Consequent to the appreciation in the exchange value of **Sterling** against other currencies, necessary fiscal measures were introduced by the government in order to reduce the likelihood of an import-led consumer spending surge.

b) Written, formal, clear.
This is clear, written English, as found in the "quality" press or in documents - even on technical subjects - aimed at ordinary educated readers.

♦ After the international value of **Sterling** rose, the government was obliged to take fiscal measures to reduce the likelihood of a surge in consumer spending led by cheaper imports.

c) Written style for the general public, discourse, scripted radio or TV news style.
This is classic English written style, as found in books, popular newspapers, and magazines for the general public. It is the style of formal discourse – discourse being spoken English from a written or "scripted" text.

♦ As the value of **Sterling** increased compared to other currencies, the government was forced to take tax measures to head off a rapid increase in consumer spending spurred on by cheaper imports.

d) Formal spoken style - radio, seminar, talk.
♦As **Sterling**'s international value went up, the government had to take tax measures to head off a consumer spending boom spurred on by cheaper imports.

e) Relaxed, informal spoken style: discussion.
There is plenty of use of **prepositional verbs.** All actions are now expressed through **verbs**, not verbal nouns.

♦ As **the Pound** went up in value, the government had to put up taxes to stop consumers splashing out on too many cheap imports.

f) Relaxed, simplified, cool, chat, very informal spoken style;
Note the addition of **repetition** and **fillers**.

♦ And you see, **the Pound** went up and up in value, so as a result the government had to go round putting up taxes, you see, to stop everyone going out and splashing out, spending all their cash on cheap imports.

5. A glossary of essential grammar terms

A list of the main terms of grammar

used to describe the words and functions of the English language

A thematic glossary of grammar terms, the words commonly used to describe points of grammar in English. The four lists below cover

1. units of meaning,
2. parts of speech,
3. structural elements and
4. general grammar terms.

The object of these lists is to explain with sufficient detail, yet as succinctly and clearly as possible, the essential vocabulary or "metalanguage" of English grammar.

5.1. Units of meaning (from big to small)

Document: A document is a written, pictural or sometimes oral, presentation of facts, fiction, ideas or opinions. It is or can be considered as complete and comprehensible in its own right.

Paragraph: Paragraphs are the principal sub-divisions of written documents. In standard descriptive or declarative documents, a paragraph is a group of sentences with the same theme. Though there is no rule, grammarians tend to agree that a paragraph will normally have between two and eight sentences, with an optimal length of 3 to 5 sentences. Longer documents may be divided into larger subdivisions such as chapters or sections or even books.

Sentence: A sentence is the basic unit that constitutes a declarative or interrogative statement. With the exception of single-word imperatives or interrogations (such as *Look!* or *What?*) or single-word answers (such as *Me.*), a sentence contains at least two words and consists of a subject and a predicate. A simple sentence contains a single clause. A compound sentence contains more than one clause.

Single word sentences can usually be considered as **ellipses**, i.e. the contraction of a longer sentences. For instance *Look!* really means something like *Look at that* or *Look at me*.

Clause: A clause is a group of words that contains a subject and a predicate. We can distinguish **main clauses**, which can stand as sentences in their own right, and **subordinate clauses** which cannot. Examples:

    Free-standing main clause: *My brother likes fast cars.*

    Two coordinated main clauses: *My brother likes fast cars, but he drives badly.*

    A main clause and a subordinate clause: *He likes cars which can go fast.*

Phrase: A phrase is a group of words which form a single unit of meaning. Examples:

    The man in the red shirt is a phrase, but so is *the red shirt* on its own.

Word: A word is the smallest complete <u>free-standing</u> unit of meaning in a language. Words come into several different categories which we call "**parts of speech**". These are detailed below.

Morpheme: A morpheme is the smallest unit of meaning in language. A word may be made up of a single lexical morpheme:

    Examples: *Give / child / speak / good / please*

or of a combination of morphemes, at least one of which must be lexical.

    Examples: *Giving / children / speaker / goodness / nationalistic*

    In the last example, *nation-al-ist-ic*, we can see four morphemes: *nation, al, ist, and ic. Nation* is a lexical morpheme or lexeme, *al ist* and *ic* are functional morphemes that cannot exist on their own, but which when attached to the lexeme serve to change its meaning or function.

A morpheme is not the same as a syllable. The word *nation* is one morpheme but two syllables

5.2. Parts of speech or grammatical categories

These descriptions are deliberately brief. Each of these parts of speech is defined and described in greater detail, with more examples, in the main part of the grammar.

Adjective: (§ 2.9) An adjective is a word that describes or modifies a noun, or occasionally a pronoun.

Examples: *Good / bad / ugly / disreputable*, as in *A big man / A good one.*

Adverb: (§ 3.1) An adverb is a word that describes of modifies a verb, an adjective, another adverb, or occasionally a whole sentence.

Examples: *Slowly / generally / upwards / somewhere / quite*

Article: (§ 2.5.) An article is a type of determiner which comes before a noun. In English we distinguish two sorts of articles, the definite article *the*, and the indefinite articles *a* and *an*. Some grammar-books also include the word *some* as an indefinite article.

Conjunction: (§ 3.3) A conjunction is a word that is used to link sentences, clauses, phrases or words. The main examples: *and / but / or / yet*. See Coordination.

Noun: (§ 2.1) A noun is a word that describes an entity (person, item, substance etc.) or a process. It is usually preceded by a determiner (article or other determiner) and may be qualified or modified by one or more adjectives, by prepositional phrases, or by another noun. Nouns are divided into two main categories, count or countable nouns, that can be counted, and non-count or uncountable nouns that cannot.

Examples: *Man / woman / chair / basket / oxygen / philosophy / idea*

Preposition: (§ 3.2) A ▶preposition is a short functional word that serves to specify meaning or relate words in terms of space, time, manner or other relation. Prepositions are essentially used to introduce a prepositional phrase (like *in the beginning*), or to inflect the meaning of a verb (like *to come in)*.

Examples: *in / on / under / against / after / with / by*

Pronoun: (§ 2.4.) A pronoun is a (usually) short word that allows a speaker or writer to refer back to an already-mentioned (or implied) noun, or to a statement, without repeating it. The main groups of pronouns are personal pronouns (*I you he she it one we they...* and their object forms or possessive forms, *me, her ...* and *mine, hers*), demonstrative pronouns (*this, that* etc.) and relative and interrogative pronouns (*who, which* etc.).

Examples: *I saw him (him* being a previously mentioned, or implied, male person*).*

or   *Yes, I heard it (it* being a previously mentioned, or implied, object such as *the bell,* event such as *the explosion,* or sentence such as *The bell rang early*).

Verb: (§ 1.0) A verb is a word that describes an action or a state of being. The verb is the key word in a sentence, and no sentence can exist without one. The shortest of all sentences consist of a single verb used in the imperative form. Example: *Look!*

There are two sorts of verbs: dynamic verbs describe actions or changes of state: examples *go / become / sit down / move;* stative verbs describe a condition or state of being: examples *be / like / know.*

5.3. Structural elements of a sentence

Subject: The subject is the main actor or the main topic of a sentence. In a basic declarative sentence, the subject comes before the verb. The subject may be just a single pronoun or noun, such as He or The cat; but in many sentences it is may be quite a bit more, including adjectives, prepositional phrases, relative clauses or more. In this example, all the words in **red** make up the subject.

Example: *The old man in the red shirt who's talking too loudly is my uncle.*

Verb: See *Verb* above.

Predicate: Everything in a sentence that is not the subject. The predicate includes the verb, or verbs, plus any other elements that may be present, notably objects or adverb phrases.

Direct Object: The **direct object** is the entity (person, thing, process) that is directly concerned by the action expressed through the verb, or is the entity that explains the action or process. It is the complement of a **transitive** verb. It can be a pronoun, a noun, a noun phrase, or more than one of these.

Examples: *I like **chocolate** /   I like **them** / I like **people who are friendly** /*

*I like **people who are friendly and don't smoke cigarettes, including you**.*

Indirect object: The **indirect object** is the person or entity that is the recipient of the action, or for whom the action is done. When the indirect object follows the direct object, it is introduced with the preposition *to*; but if it precedes the direct object, *to* is omitted.

Examples: *I gave a bone **to the dog***

*I gave **the dog** a bone / I gave **it** a bone.*

Main clause: The main clause is the principal clause in a sentence. There can be one main clause or more in a sentence; if there is more than one main clause, these will be separated by a semi-colon (;), or by a coordinating conjunction such as *and, but* or *yet*.

A **subordinate or dependent clause** cannot exist without a main clause. It is normally introduced by a subordinating conjunction, such as *since, if, because* or *as,* or by a relative pronoun such as *who* or *that*.

Examples: *You can go home now **if you've finished your project.***

***As I said,** there are no tickets left for the concert.*

***When he reached Manchester**, he looked for a hotel.*

*I know three people **who live in Boston.***

5.4. Other grammatical terms A-Z

Active: In English, most statements are made using the **active** voice. In an active statement, the **subject** is the doer of the action expressed by means of the verb. For example *The students were studying English*.

Antecedent: the word or phrase to which a **pronoun** refers. In most cases the antecedent comes before the pronoun, but in questions (such is *Is it a problem?*) it may follow.

Apposition: Normally a direct sequence of two nouns, with no intervening preposition, which both refer to the same entity:

Examples: *Prince William / The car, a Jaguar,...*

The painting, a work by Rembrandt,....

In English, except in titles (such as *Doctor Jekyll*), the second or "apposed" noun requires a determiner, normally an article. Apposition should not be confused with compound nouns, in which two nouns placed next to each other refer to different things; for example *The shop window.*

Aspect: In English, verbs can be expressed in two aspects, the **simple** aspect (such as *I drink*) or the **progressive** aspect (such as *I am drinking*).

Attributive: An adjective that is **attributive** is one that is placed in front of the noun it qualifies (as in *A good book*).Contrast with adjectives following a copular verb such as *be* , which are called predicative adjectives (as in *This book is good*).

Auxiliary: A helper verb that comes before a main verb to designate a tense, a modality or the passive voice. The basic auxiliaries are *be* and *have*: modal auxiliaries are *will, shall, may, might, must, can, be able to* and their other forms.

Catenative verbs or **consecutive verbs**. Verbs that can be followed directly by a second verb, with no intervening noun or pronoun (as in *I like playing football*). See *Consecutive verbs.*

Communication: The object of speech or writing. Communication cannot be successful unless the **producer** (speaker, writer) and the **receiver** (listener, reader) are using the same language **code**. The code consists of two elements: vocabulary (words) and grammar (how those words are organised).

Comparative: A particular meaning that is given to an adjective or adverb either by adding *-er* to the end of an adjective, or by adding *more* before an adjective or adverb.

Complement:: The main element of the predicate after a copular verb. See *object* above, see *copular verb* below.

Conjunctive adverb: A type of **connector**, a type of *sentence adverb* used to express a particular relationship between a first clause and a second clause that follows. Examples: *Therefore, however, similarly.*   See *Conjunctive adverbs (§ 3.4).*

Connector: A word that links two similar items (words, phrases, clauses). Connectors are either conjunctions or conjunctive adverbs. See conjunctions

Coordination: Linking two or more elements with similar status in the sentence.

Copular verb: A verb whose **complement** is not an object, but a description of the subject. Examples: *The car is red, I feel sick, The children became very excited*.

Declarative: A declarative sentence is a normal sentence, which is neither an interrogative sentence (question), nor an exclamation, nor an imperative. A declarative sentence can be affirmative or negative.

Examples: *The man is sitting on a chair*, and *The man is not sitting on a chair* are both declarative statements.

Determiner: **Determiners** are used at the start of a noun phrase. The most common determiners are articles; but determiners also include demonstratives, numerals, or possessive determiners. All nouns or noun phrases require a determiner unless they are used as generalisations.

Examples: *The man is eating his dinner,*
and *That man is eating chips*.

No determiner is required before *chips*, which is used as a generalisation. For more on this, see count and non-count nouns

Discourse marker: A word or phrase, usually a conjunctive adverb, a filler or a free-standing adverb, which indicates the relation of one sentence or phrase to the next.

Ellipsis: A statement that is reduced to a minimum number of words, by the elimination of words whose meaning can be implied or inferred. For example *the man in the garden* can be understood as an ellipsis of *the man who is in the garden*. Or the simple expression *London* can exist as an **elliptical** sentence in reply to the question *Where do you live?* – the elliptical sentence implying the meaning *I live in London*.

Endings: Also called suffixes, endings are grammatical or functional morphemes that are added to the end of word to inflect or change its meaning. Compared to many languages, English has relatively few endings. There are actually only three common endings in English that are used to make inflected forms of a word, without changing its category. These are *-ing, -ed,* and *-s* for verbs, and *-s* for nouns. Other endings are used to change the grammatical category of a word, for example *-ness* or *-ity* that form nouns from adjectives, or *-ful or -less* that form adjectives from nouns.

Gerund: A Gerund is a type of *-ing word*. To distinguish gerunds from present participles, see § *1.9 Gerunds.*

Gradable: Adjectives are called **gradable** if they can be modified by an **intensifier** such as *very, quite or extremely*. Most adjectives are gradable, but some are not. For example we can say *A rather expensive car* or *The children became very excited*, but we cannot say

~~John has a very electric car.~~ A car is electric, or it is not electric. It cannot be *very electric*, or *quite electric*.

Grammar: The corpus of rules and principles that describe how a language is used or should be used. Grammar can be **prescriptive** (telling people what is correct and what is not) , or **descriptive** (describing what how people actually use language). Grammar is constantly evolving, but it does so more slowly that vocabulary. As well as traditional grammar, linguists have developed other types of grammar to better analyse language, such as transformational grammar, cognitive grammar, or generative grammar.

Imperative: The form of the verb that we use when we give an order or a command. See Imperative.

Indicative: In English, almost all verbs are used in the indicative mood. The subjunctive, the other principal mood, is rare.

Intensifier: A type of adverb that is used to give extra force to the meaning of an adjective. Examples: *very / extremely / most / highly.*

Metalanguage: In linguistics, the words and expressions used to describe language itself. The expressions explained on this page are the essential terms used to describe language in English.

Modal verb: Modal verbs, or modal auxiliaries, such as *can* or *must*, are used to express possibility, obligation, probability or futurity. See § 1.15 Modals of obligation, *§ 1.16 Modals of possibility* , *§ 1.3 Expressing the future.*

Modify: In grammar, the word *modify* most commonly means to give a specific meaning to a noun or verb. Modifiers include adjectives, adverbs and prepositional phrases

Mood: In English there are three moods, the **indicative,** the **subjunctive** and the **indicative**. The subjunctive is very rarely used.

Morpheme: A distinct element of meaning. For example the word *unthinkable* contains three morphemes, *un, think,* and *able*. The word *elephant* contains just one morpheme.

Morphology: the study of the structure of words

Passive: A passive sentence is one in which the subject is the topic of the action, not the actor or agent. See *§ 1.8 The passive voice.*

>Example: *The tree was blown over by the wind.* In this example, the actor or agent of the action is *the wind.*

Predicate: One of the two essential constituents of a sentence, the other one being the **subject**. The predicate is made up of everything in the sentence that is not contained in the subject. In a normal affirmative sentence, it follows the subject. It must contain a verb.

Punctuation: An aspect of syntax, punctuation consists of a small number of symbols that are used to delimit, when necessary, words, phrases or sentences. See § 4.7 Punctuation

Quantifier: A quantifier is a type of **determiner** that expresses an imprecise or undefined quantity; it can be contrasted with a number that expresses a precise quantity. Quantifiers include words such as *some, many, a few, several*. See § 2.6. Quantifiers

Relative: A relative clause is a clause introduced by a relative pronoun such as *who, which, whose* etc.

Semantics: the study of meaning. Semantic analysis can be applied either to words or to the elements, such as prefixes or suffixes, of which words are made up .

Subject: The actor or topic of a sentence. In a simple sentence, the subject comes first, before the predicate.

Subordination: see *subordinate clause* above.

Suffix: A morpheme (element of meaning) added to the end of a word. See *endings* above.

Style: The manner in which ideas are expressed as words. Style can be anything from formal to informal, or oral to written. See *§ 4.9. Style in English.*

Superlative: The highest degree of an adjective or adverb. Superlatives are formed either by adding *-est* to an adjective, or by adding the word *most* before an adjective or an adverb.

Syllable: In phonetics, a unit of sound. Some words are monosyllables, with just one unit of sound, for example *I, egg, boy, this, stand;* other words are made up of two or more syllables, for example *nation, basket, given, complicated.*

Syntax: An aspect of grammar, syntax deals with the way in which words are organised and ordered. It includes word order and punctuation.

Tense: Tenses are specific forms of verbs which are used to situate an action in time. According to a current convention in modern linguistics, English just has two tenses, as defined by **morphological** criteria – the present tense and the past tense; but this is just one way of classifying tenses in English, and not necessarily the most logical way.

For purposes of simplicity and clarity, many books and language teachers use the word *tense* in a much broader sense, as a **semantic** category, in which a tense is the form of a verb used to denote a particular time frame – as is accepted practice for languages like French Spanish or Russian.

It is important to understand that there is no absolute truth. Saying that there are two tenses in English is not any more accurate, nor more exact, than saying there are six tenses, or even twelve tenses, as many eminent grammarians have done in the past. It depends on the criteria – morphological or semantic – used to define the notion of "tense".

English verbs come in different forms and different aspects, so for example in the two-tense model, the English present **tense** is a single tense with four **forms**, the present simple and the present progressive, the present perfect simple and the present perfect progressive. In the six-tense model, these are six different tenses, each with two aspects; and in the twelve-tense model, there are twelve tenses.

Transitive: Verbs are either **transitive** or **intransitive**. Some verbs are always one or the other, some verbs can be either depending on their use. A transitive verb is a verb that must have a direct object.

> Example: *The dog was barking / The dog was eating a bone*

In the first example, *barking* is intransitive. It cannot take an object. In the second example, *eating* is used transitively, because there is an object *bone*. The verb *eat* can also be used intransitively, i.e. with no object, as in: *The dog was eating*.

Voice: A key factor describing the way in which a verb is used. There are two voices, the **active** and the **passive**. See *verbs*.

Appendix

Alphabetical list of 80 common consecutive verbs

- Note that apart from **allow**, used as an example, the table below does not include verbs of authority (permit, forbid, let), modal verbs, or non-consecutive verbs.

In this table, each verb is listed in the form of a short and realistic example.

Verb, in sample form	Type	followed by a gerund (-ing).	followed by an infinitive with to	Notes
He admitted		doing it *or* <u>to</u> doing it		
He advised	1	taking the train.	**us** to take the train	Depends on the structure
I can afford	1	(rare)	to buy a new car	Gerund sometimes used in negative structures
I agreed	1		to meet him at 8.	
I aim	1		to finish on time	
I allow	1		**you** to go home now.	Can only be used without an object in the passive
I appreciate	2	being here.		
I arranged	1		to meet him.	
She asked	1		to go home.	
She attempted	1		to hide.	
I avoid	2	travelling on busy days		
I can't bear	2	living in London	to be without you.	Slightly different meanings.
He begged	1		to stay.	
I begin		(rare)	to understand.	
He didn't bother		telling anyone	to tell anyone.	Either structure is possible
I choose	1		to remain silent.	
She completed		filling in the form.		
She consented			to marry him.	
She considered		going to South Africa.		
He continued	2	living in London	to live in London.	The same meaning.

But!! He went on	2	living in London	to live in London.	Take care! Two **different** meanings
He dares	1		to argue with me.	or: argue with me.
He decided	1		to stop smoking.	
I delayed		going to New York.		
To deny		having been present.		
He deserves	1		to be punished.	
I detest	2	eating fish.		
I dislike	2	eating fish.		
I enjoy	2	eating fish.		
I expect	1		to win first prize.	
He failed			to win a prize.	
He finished		building the wall.		
She forget			to say she was going home.	
I am going	1	swimming.	to swim.	Take care! Slightly **different** meanings
He happened			to hear her.	
He helped			to paint the garage.	Take care! Also ..paint the garage.
I couldn't help		hearing what you said.		Take care!
I hesitate	1		to do that.	
I hope	1		to be there	
He imagined	2	living in Tahiti.		
I intend	1		to be there.	
He will learn			to speak English	
I like or love	2	being with you	to be with you	Either structure possible
But!! I would like	2	living in London	to live in London.	Take care! Slightly **different** meanings
I long	1		to be with you.	
It means	2	starting again.		Take care! in the sense of *implies*
He means	1		to start again	Take care! in the sense of *plans*
I don't mind	2	living in London.		
I miss	2	seeing you.		
He neglected			to say he was going out.	
He offered	1		to help	

I plan	1	being here by 8.	to be here by 8.	The gerund form is not common
She practises		singing all day.		
I prefer	2	living here	to go by train.	
They prepared	1		to welcome the Queen.	
I pretended			to laugh.	
She proceeded (went on)	1		to win the match.	
I promise	1		to be good.	
I propose	1	staying here	to go home.	Depends on the context.
I recall		living in London.		
I recommend		seeing this film	**you** to see this film	Depends on the context.
He refused	1		to change his mind.	
I remembered		living in London.	to shut the door.	Take care! **Different** meanings.
I regret	2	having done that.		
I resumed		reading my book.		
She risked		being seen.		
It seems			to be OK.	
I can't stand	2	living in London.		
I started		reading.	to read.	Either structure possible
I stopped		reading.	to have a drink.	Take care! Two **different** meanings
I suggest		going home now.		
I swear	1		to tell the truth.	
I tend			to agree with you.	
He threatened	1		to hit me.	
Will you try		opening this for me!	to open it?	Slightly different meanings
He undertakes	1		to finish it by midnight.	
I'm waiting	1		to go home.	
I want	2	to go home.		
I wish	2	to go home.		

www.ingramcontent.com/pod-product-compliance
Lightning Source LLC
LaVergne TN
LVHW050843080526
838202LV00009B/322